FOR LIFE-GIV

THE ART OF SPIRITUAL LEADERSHIP

HABITUDES®

IMAGES
THAT FORM
LEADERSHIP
HABITS &
ATTITUDES

BY
DR TIM
ELMORE

PUBLISHED IN ATLANTA, GEORGIA BY GROWING LEADERS, INC.
(WWW.GROWINGLEADERS.COM)

ISBN: 978-1-7320703-3-2

PRINTED IN THE UNITED STATES OF AMERICA

LIBRARY OF CONGRESS CATALOGUING-IN-PUBLICATION DATA

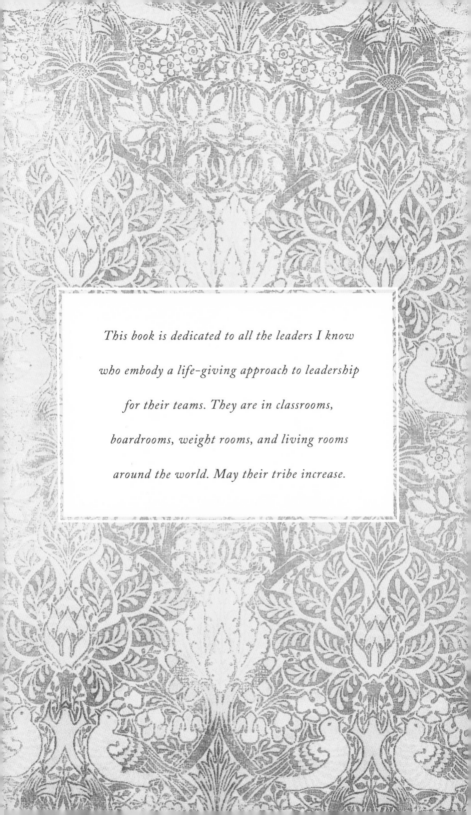

This book is dedicated to all the leaders I know

who embody a life-giving approach to leadership

for their teams. They are in classrooms,

boardrooms, weight rooms, and living rooms

around the world. May their tribe increase.

TABLE OF CONTENTS

★

*Available exclusively in
Habitudes for Life-Giving Leaders: The Art of Spiritual Leadership

A WORD ABOUT IMAGES

We live in a culture rich with images. We grew up with photographs, TV, movies, video, MTV and DVDs. We can't escape the power of the visual image—and most of us don't want to.

I've learned over my career that most of us are visual learners. We like to see a picture, not just hear a word. Author Leonard Sweet says that images are the language of the 21st century, not words. Some of the best communicators in history taught using the power of the metaphor and image—from Jesus Christ and His parables to Martin Luther King Jr. and his "I Have a Dream" speech, during the Civil Rights movement. "The best leaders," writes Tom Peters, "...almost without exception and at every level, are master users of stories and symbols."

Why? Because pictures stick. We remember pictures long after words have left us. When we hear a speech, we often remember the stories from that speech, more than the phrases used by the speaker, because they painted a picture inside of us. They communicate far more than mere words. In fact, words are helpful only as they conjure up a picture in our minds. Most of us think in pictures. If I say the word "elephant" to you, you don't picture the letters: e-l-e-p-h-a-n-t. You picture a big gray animal. Pictures are what we file away in our minds. They enable us to store huge volumes of information. There's an old phrase that has stood the test of time: A picture is worth a thousand words. I believe it's true. While studying commercial art in college I recognized the power of the image. Now I get to combine the power of teaching leadership truths with the power of pictures. I hope they linger in your mind and heart. I hope you discover layers of reality in them, as you grow in your leadership skills. I trust they'll impact you profoundly as they have me.

This Particular Book
The purpose of this particular resource is to offer you a picture of what I believe a leader should look like as they fully mature. Its very different than the image we frequently see in leaders today who seek power and count "likes" and "views" on social media. In contrast, this leader is life-giving. Life-giving leaders are all about people and causes that are outside of themselves. The book illustrates a new kind of leader's lifestyle. While it contains both life-giving habits and attitudes—much of this book is about a leader's approach and attitudes about what it means to influence a team of people.

I believe the best leaders are not merely transactional in nature. They are transformational. They breathe life on others, inspiring them to perform in a better way than they could have without that leader. A life-giving leader brings out the best in people by believing the best about people.

They take the high road and influence others to do the same. They change the culture of the organization or team they lead because of the way they carry themselves and by the way they interact with their team.

- THEY INSPIRE
- THEY BELIEVE
- THEY LISTEN
- THEY STRENGTHEN
- THEY MOTIVATE
- THEY EMPOWER

Some sociologists describe this generation as EPIC: Experiential, Participatory, Image-driven and Connected. If that's true, I believe we'll get the most out of resources that give us an image, an experience and a way to connect with each other. Each of these books provides you not only with an image, but a handful of stories, questions, a self-assessment and an exercise in which you can participate. Dive in and experience each one of them. My hope is that they become signposts that guide you, and warn you and inform you on your leadership journey.

Dr. Tim Elmore

Quarterbacks and Referees

ALL FOOTBALL GAMES HAVE QUARTERBACKS WHO PROVIDE DIRECTION, INSPIRE AND DEPLOY THE TEAM. THE REFEREES ARE THERE TO ENFORCE THE RULES OF THE GAME, WATCH THE BOUNDARIES AND CALL FOULS. NO ONE ATTENDS A FOOTBALL GAME TO SEE A REFEREE. LIFE-GIVING LEADERS FIGHT THE TENDENCY TO MERELY REFEREE. THEY ARE THE QUARTERBACKS.

I love watching college and professional football. Because our organization, Growing Leaders, serves so many teams in the NCAA and NFL, I get the chance to meet coaches and players from all over the country and watch plenty of games.

After recently witnessing an incredible game, I started thinking about what attracted me so much to this sport. It's a potent combination of strength and strategy. It's about managing the clock, blending the talent on a team, and using every tool available to your advantage. In fact, it's very difficult to win consistently without good leadership on a football team.

It dawned on me that every competition actually has two leaders on the field who are essential to the flow and the outcome of the game, yet we rarely compare them. There is one that we want to watch and one we don't pay much attention to: the quarterback and the referee.

TWO KINDS OF LEADERS IN FOOTBALL

If you think about it, referees are essential because the results of so many plays on the gridiron are debatable. We need those folks with the striped shirts to watch each play closely and blow the whistle when they believe it's over. Especially on close plays, both teams trust referees to maintain order on the field. Without referees who would decide if a pass is incomplete? Who would prevent a late hit? How would we know if the running back breaks the plain and scores a touchdown? In many ways, referees offer a necessary piece of leadership that protects the integrity of the game.

Quarterbacks are a much different kind of leader. The good ones are incredible to watch. They are smart, agile, and can see everything on the field (much like a good referee). But, quarterbacks are all about moving the ball toward the end zone: passing, running, or handing it off so their team can score. Over a career, good quarterbacks display how important it is to leverage the talent around them to win. The great quarterbacks like Joe Namath, Roger Staubach, Joe Montana, Troy Aikman, John Elway, Peyton Manning, Tom Brady, or Cam Newton make everyone around them perform better.

When I pause to reflect, it's clear the game needs both quarterbacks and referees. But, there's a big difference. A referee is not central to the meaning of the game. No one ever attends a football game to watch the referee.

LESSONS FROM THE PLAYING FIELD

As I've watched leaders over the years, I have noticed a pattern. We often begin our careers like a quarterback: we're inspiring, we've got ideas, we have the vision to make progress for our organization. Over time, however, we often begin to look more like a referee. Our work becomes more about calling people out when we believe they're out of bounds or blowing the whistle when we see something wrong. When our focus in life becomes more about compliance to rules than accomplishing a mission, we might as well put on a striped shirt.

This comparison of the referee and the quarterback is too important to miss. The shift we make from relationships to regulations can be both subtle and frightening. Life-giving leaders are entrepreneurial and, therefore, very attractive. Even when their organization is well established, they remain innovative and passionate. Sadly, too many leaders spiral into a lifeless routine of officiating within a few years. They can even become repulsive. Note the contrast below:

REFEREES	QUARTERBACKS
1. Calling penalties	1. Making progress
2. Information	2. Inspiration
3. Counting players on the field	3. Empowering players on the field
4. All about downs and rules	4. All about delegation and results
5. Keeping the ball in bounds	5. Moving the ball forward
6. Aim is to control the plays	6. Aim is to connect with players
7. The goal is maintenance	7. The goal is the mission

My friend, Greg, began as a ministry leader right out of college. He worked with students for five years before his supervisor promoted him to take on larger roles. Over time, I noticed that Greg's style of leadership was changing. No doubt, he was becoming a stronger leader—but I noticed he was also losing perspective on why he chose to serve in the first place.

Greg smiled less, marveled less, and risked less. After ten years, I could hardly recognize him. As we met for accountability, Greg eventually acknowledged what I was observing. He had become a referee. He was guarding more than guiding; he was controlling more than connecting. It's the easiest trap to fall into as a ministry leader. The shift is slow, subtle, and sinister.

How People Respond When Led by a Referee

No doubt, every organization, just like every good football game, needs referees. In fact, the larger your organization, the more you truly need them. Someone must watch the details, establish systems and processes, and set strong boundaries. I'm speaking, however, about a mindset. Even the leaders whose jobs are to keep things in-bounds can do so (can referee) with the heart of a quarterback. When we don't, we are the ones who lose.

For years, surveys have reported that members of the youngest generation of adults in the U.S. are far less likely than older Americans to identify with a religious group. Sadly, a 2015 Pew Research Center survey found that, as time goes on, the immense share of religiously unaffiliated Millennials is steadily increasing. A high percentage of younger members—those I call "Generation iY," who were born since 1990—are religious "nones" (self-proclaimed atheists or agnostics, or their religion is "nothing in particular"). At the same time, an increasing share of older Millennials also identify as nones, with more members of that group rejecting religious labels. I actually know a young woman who planned to become a nun but instead became a "none."

The shrinking number of Christians is the most significant change since 2007 (when Pew did its first U.S. Religious Landscape Study). In short, young adults are leaving organized ministries in droves.[1]

"In many cases, those who left the church didn't stop believing, they just stopped attending," my friend Andy Stanley said. It wasn't God who turned them off—it was their leader. They perceive these Christian leaders as "referees" who keep score, watch boundaries and call penalties—leaders who offer regulation instead of inspiration.

They're known more for what they're against, than what they are for. They start looking more like Pharisees than Jesus. The Pharisees' ethics were about avoidance. Jesus' ethic was about involvement. Maybe David Eddy said it best when he proclaimed, "God save us from religion."

What Quarterback Leadership Looks Like

In 2015, Disney released a movie called "McFarland USA." It's based on the true story of Jim White, an ordained minister who chose to serve at McFarland High School in a Hispanic farming town in California's Central Valley. In the 1980s, the area was filled with kids who were destined to work in the fields around town. The area was depressed: kids broke rules, were suspended, and many were hopeless.

It was a town where adults found it easy to suspect the worst from teens—assume they'd do drugs, become thieves, or live dead-end lives. In short, the goal for many adults was to referee—just keep the kids in bounds. Instead of taking a job at a church, White chose to launch his ministry as a teacher and track coach. He wasn't a runner himself and had never coached a track team, but he saw this as a chance to build good men by leading the very first cross-country team in school history.

You probably know the rest of the story. Jim and his wife, Sheryl, lived out their faith in front of the teens. They hugged their sweaty bodies after practice, fed them, bought them shoes, and took several to the beach for the very first time. Rather than focusing on the wrong those teens had done, they painted a picture of what could be: not only college, but a scholarship to college. Not just a job, but a career. Not just a religion, but a relationship with Christ for them and their future families.

In the end, these teens who'd never competed as track athletes won nine state championships. White's leadership secret? He was a quarterback in a world of referees.

"I hoped they could see God through us," White said.

LOOK AT THE BOOK: REFLECT AND RESPOND

God's sharpest anger is expressed toward leaders who get this issue wrong. Study the following passages and draw some conclusions yourself:

1. Read Jeremiah 23:1-4. Exactly, why is God disappointed? How will he respond?

   _____

   _____

2. Read Matthew 23:1-12. Discuss the leadership problems listed. What were they?

   _____

   _____

3. Read the "seven woes" of Matthew 23:13-36. Do you see applications for us today?

   _____

   _____

Comedian Lenny Bruce said, "Every day people are straying away from the church and going back to God." What a sad commentary. Sometimes, it can be our fault. Philip Keller warns us with his statement, "The greatest threat to the church today is not from without, but from our own leadership within." Often, an abusive ministry is built around a leader who practices unhealthy forms of shepherding. Many such leaders arise from ministries that were abusive or they have an unmet need for significance. Many begin with noble intentions, but their unresolved personal issues cause them to become dependent on their ministry to meet their needs. So, evaluate yourself:

1. In what areas of your leadership would others say you're more like a referee?

   Being a big brother, ~~teacher~~ referee in cross

2. Have you seen yourself migrate from being a quarterback to a referee? How did it happen? When did it happen?

   I dont know when, but definity during cross country with all the freshman

3. When you practice unhealthy leadership, can you put your finger on why?

   No

4. Score yourself on a scale of 1-5, with one being "never" and five being "always":

   Do you use your position to demand loyalty?
   NEVER> 1   (2)   3   4   5 <ALWAYS

   Do you use your position to avoid accountability?
   NEVER> 1   2   (3)   4   5 <ALWAYS

   Do you use your position to manipulate behavior?
   NEVER> 1   (2)   3   4   5 <ALWAYS

   Do you use your position to induce guilt?
   NEVER> 1   2   (3)   4   5 <ALWAYS

Do you use your position to coerce people to donate or serve?

NEVER> 1 ② 3 4 5 <ALWAYS

Now, talk over your responses with colleagues. What changes are needed?

_____

_____

TRY IT OUT: PRACTICING THE TRUTH

When we stop and reflect, almost every interaction a person has with the "law" is a negative one. Not once have I seen a referee throw a flag onto the field to affirm the talent of the players. It's always about a penalty. And never have I seen a police officer pull over a driver to compliment them on the way they handle their car. Nope. It's almost always to offer a citation. This is what we expect. Unfortunately, the same reputation can surface with a person in any type of leadership role.

This week, ask at least three people who interact with you regularly to honestly evaluate their perception of your leadership. How do people view you as a leader of your club, team, class, or peers? When you approach them, do they suspect something negative has happened? Talk it over.

Then, try this habit. In every interaction you have this week, practice the following:

- INITIATE CONTACT WITH THE OTHER PERSON INSTEAD OF WAITING FOR THEM TO MAKE THE FIRST MOVE.

- FIND SOMETHING GOOD TO AFFIRM IN THE PERSON. CONNECT WITH THEM.

- OFFER A GIFT, A CONSTRUCTIVE COMMENT OR WORD OF AFFIRMATION. ADD VALUE.

- PROVIDE SOME POSITIVE DIRECTION IF THEY NEED IT. BREATHE LIFE INTO THEM.

After one week, reflect on your experience. How did your interactions differ from past ones?

Three Buckets

EVERYTHING THAT HAPPENS TO A LEADER FALLS INTO ONE OF THREE "BUCKETS:" WHAT IS IN THEIR CONTROL, WHAT IS OUT OF THEIR CONTROL, OR WHAT IS WITHIN THEIR INFLUENCE. HEALTHY, LIFE-GIVING LEADERS EFFECTIVELY PLACE EACH EXPERIENCE IN THE CORRECT BUCKET AND ACT ACCORDINGLY: INITIATE, TRUST, OR RESPOND.

When I began my career in 1979 serving students in a church ministry, my heart was in the right place. I didn't know much, but I sure had pure motives. I didn't have much wisdom or experience, but I did have a lot of passion.

My first youth group included three students: Ralph, Becky, and Keith. I served as a part-time youth pastor while I worked on my bachelor's degree. When I finished four years later, the group had grown to 60 students each week. We'd made some progress.

At that point, I moved to San Diego, California, to join the staff of Dr. John C. Maxwell. While I was still teaching students, I began to recognize the importance of leadership development. I started to invest time into training student leaders and saw our department increase from an average of 60 students each week to an average of 600 young adults in two classes each week. It was fun to see that growth occur.

But something else happened for which I was not prepared.

I became more controlling. The evolution of my demeanor and my motives were subtle, but real. At first, I trusted God and my volunteers entirely for everything. I had to because I was young and had nothing else to go on except trust and hope. As time marched on, however, I slowly drifted into wanting to control of our program and all the results. Unwittingly, I wanted to control the inputs and the outcomes. Success can be addictive. I sought to engineer every minute of our meetings, to command every line of our budget and to force progress. After all, I was the leader.

One afternoon, one of the kindest, most respectful college students in our department sat in my office and said to me, "You know, I love our department, but it seems like you're trying to control everything."

Like many others, this young woman was suffocating under my controlling leadership style.

She then asked me, "Have you observed this, too?"

I had not. In fact, I was offended.

It wasn't until later that I gained perspective about what this student had noticed. It's not that I was a bad person. I wasn't robbing banks or committing adultery or even lying or cheating. I simply had swapped jobs with God. I wanted to control things, and prayed that he would trust me with the reins of my ministry.

Understanding the Three Buckets

What I learned from that season of my career was simple: When I was in control, I had the best ministry that human effort could build. But, I wanted more than that; I wanted the best that God could create. Big difference. Since that time, I've come to believe that every experience we have serving God falls into one of three buckets:

- It is in my control
- It is out of my control
- It is within my influence

Power is a strange thing. When we serve well, we tend to accrue it as a byproduct. Eventually, however, we shift our pursuit. We bypass the essential acts of service and begin yearning directly for the power. It's so easy to do. We see it on TV every week. It's that preacher who, at first, believes it's all about making God famous. Over time, however, it becomes about selling his products and making himself famous.

Problems arise when we do not understand what is in our control, what is out of our control, and what is within our influence. When we assess our situations wrong, when we place them in the wrong bucket, it can lead to conflict, distrust, stalls, and turmoil. The secret to good leadership to place every situation in the right context or bucket. Items placed in the wrong bucket will prevent us from being life-giving leaders and can lead to an obsession with power and control.

"Power tends to corrupt," 19th century British historian Lord Acton said. "Absolute power corrupts absolutely."

His axiom has been vividly displayed in psychological studies over the years, most memorably the 1971 Stanford Prison Experiment, which was terminated when one group of students arbitrarily assigned to serve as prison guards over another group began to abuse their prisoners.

Placing our Experiences in the Right Buckets and Responding Well

My life and leadership has been liberated since learning to place relationships and events in the proper buckets. When I do, I assume my intended role and allow God to take his proper role. Here is a summary of how leaders must respond:

Bucket One: "It is in my control. I must initiate."

Our response should be to take responsibility. If something is in my control, I must flee the temptation to avoid action or find a scapegoat to blame when things go wrong. God works in partnership with leaders, and offers us roles to play. We must not become like Moses and make excuses. We must not become like Adam and blame Eve. We must initiate and take proper responsibility. It's up to us to lead the way.

Bucket Two: "It is out of my control. I must trust."

Our response in these circumstances is to trust. We can't force others to obey us. We can't heal anyone who's sick or conjure up money. For that matter, we can't perform any miracle at all. We must trust God for what he alone can do. We must not become like Sarah and manipulate, nor become like Nebuchadnezzar and dominate. In this case, we must trust the plan he has for us, and remain steady and faithful.

Bucket Three: It is within my influence. I must respond wisely.

Our response in this third bucket requires wisdom. It is a mixture of the first two buckets. We can't control the situation, but we can influence it. We can't force others to give or volunteer, but we can challenge them. We can't make people love us, but we can love them first and seek their response. We must not become like Pilate and avoid action; we must not become like Jonah and run. It's a dance. It's a volley.

Case Study: David and Uriah

In 2 Samuel 11, we read a vivid case study of two leaders: one who gets this right and one who gets it wrong. King David, a hero of our faith, has come into power. He's succeeded at almost everything he set his hand to do. In that spring season, it was the time when kings went to battle with their armies and led the way for their men—it was what good leaders did. David, however, stayed home and remained idle. (**He got bucket one wrong**).

One evening, while walking on his rooftop, he noticed his neighbor's wife, Bathsheba, bathing next door. Her husband, Uriah, was out on the battle lines, so she was alone. She looked beautiful to David, so he summoned her to his home. He couldn't resist trying to meet his need for intimacy his own way. Even though he had his own wives, he wanted her. Instead of trusting, David is into taking. Months later, Bathsheba discovered that she was pregnant with David's baby. (**He got bucket two wrong**).

Next, David attempted to control the consequences of his errors. He called for Uriah to come home and meet with him. King David got him drunk and encouraged him to go spend the night with his wife. After all, he deserved it But, alas, Uriah felt he should not enjoy a night with his wife while his comrades were on the battlefield. So, he slept at the entrance of the palace. His conscience would not let him skirt his duty. When David sent him back into battle, he sent along a sealed note, telling his officer, Joab, to put Uriah on the front lines of battle and make sure he was struck down. David actually abused his influence as a leader. **(He got bucket three wrong).**

Getting these buckets right is crucial for leaders. Uriah took control of responsibilities that were in his control—showing up for battle and returning at the king's request. He trusted God with items out of his control—taking the king's note to his captain, even though it was his death sentence. Finally, he handled items in his influence by letting his conscience guide him to sleep on the steps of the palace instead of indulging in the luxury of seeing his wife. Uriah placed every experience in the right bucket. David misplaced them all.

During that season of their careers, Uriah, while drunk, was a better man than David, while sober.

Science Confirms It...
Current studies from UC Berkeley on the science of power confirm a biblical truth: power is wielded most effectively when used responsibly by people who are attuned and engaged with the needs of others.

Years of research confirm that empathy and social intelligence are vastly more important than acquiring power through manipulation, intimidation or deception. Sadly, these studies also show that once people obtain some power, most tend to act more selfishly. (*Greater Good Science Center, UCB*). The fact is, a 2012 study found that power doesn't corrupt, but it heightens preexisting ethical tendencies.[2] Control freaks beware: power causes us to become more of who we already are.

Don't Create the Wave, Ride It

My friend Roy Otto spoke to me about this control issue once, comparing it to surfing. Having lived in San Diego for years, this made sense to me. When surfers wade into the ocean, their job is not to create the waves. They simply spot them and ride them into the shore. The ocean makes them. The surfer rides them. And so it is with us. We are not called to create the wave. Only God can genuinely do that. We are to see the waves he's created and hop on. Let him do his role, and be sure to get onboard. And be sure to take your three buckets with you. Whether you feel stressed or blessed will likely depend on how you handle these buckets.

Look at the Book: Reflect and Respond

This truth is evident throughout the scriptures. With the three buckets in mind, review the following passages and jot down the right responses:

1. Read Genesis 3:1-19. What should Adam have done instead of refusing to lead Eve?

   _____

   _____

2. Read Genesis 16:1-6. What should Sarah have done instead of manipulating Hagar?

   _____

   _____

3. Read Matthew 27:11-26. How should Pilate have led instead of washing his hands?

   _____

   _____

Assess Yourself

When you reflect on the three buckets, list areas where you can grow the most:

1. In what area of your leadership would others say you're controlling?

   _____

   _____

2. In what area of your leadership would others say you pass the buck?

   _____

   _____

3. In what area of your leadership have you failed to influence wisely?

   _____

   _____

Rate Yourself

Circle your most accurate response on each line in these two columns below:

Wrong Buckets

1. I pursue control over people
2. I utilize manipulation and power
3. I tend to languish in uncertainty
4. I enforce policies
5. I am cowardly in difficult times

Right Buckets

1. I pursue connection with people
2. I leverage mission and passion
3. I tend to lead clearly in certainty
3. I empower people
4. I am courageous in difficult times

Try it Out: Practicing the Truth

This week, consciously make the following shifts as you influence people:

1. Don't think **control**. Think *connect*.
2. Don't leverage **positional power**. Leverage *personal power*.
3. Don't ask, "What can I **gain**?" Instead, ask, "What can I *give*?"
4. Don't pursue **rights**. Pursue *responsibilities*.
5. Don't fight for **turf**. Fight for *trust*.
6. Don't lead by **telling**. Lead with *asking*.

After practicing these mindset shifts for a week, how did your approach to life and leadership change? Discuss these changes.

Root and Fruit

A HEALTHY TREE HAS UNSEEN ROOTS THAT STABILIZE IT AGAINST THE ELEMENTS, A TRUNK TO GIVE IT HEIGHT AND NOURISHMENT AND FRUIT TO SUBSTANTIATE ITS VALUE. LIFE-GIVING LEADERS PRIORITIZE THEIR GROWTH ELEMENTS IN THIS SAME ORDER. IT'S ABOUT "WHO" BEFORE "WHAT."

I'm no horticulturist, but I've seen some amazing plants and trees in my lifetime. For years, I lived in California, home of the famous redwood trees. I also lived in Colorado, where beautiful evergreen trees flourish in the mountains. I now reside in the South, where much of the year, you can see the lush foliage of dogwood trees, southern magnolias, and sugar maple trees. I've noticed trees have personalities just like people do. For example, there is a look, a feel, and a style you'll experience as you observe a weeping willow that is so different from that of a pine tree.

Years ago, I remember hiking in Hawaii while on vacation. My family had chosen to leave the "touristy" parts of Honolulu and see portions of the island most travelers never get to see. While near the coast, I stumbled upon a tree growing on a cliff. Because of how it was positioned at the edge of the cliff, you could not only observe its trunk and branches, but also see that the roots were exposed. I could literally examine the entire tree, below and above the ground.

This moment was an educational experience for me.

LESSONS FROM THE ROOT AND FRUIT OF TREES

The role of each part of that tree became tangibly clear and vividly important. While we rarely get to see the roots of a tree, they provide the foundation for the strength, stabilization, and life of the tree. The deeper they go, the taller it can grow. The wider they reach out beneath the ground, the more the wind can blow without taking the tree down. The strongest trees have roots that are both deep and wide. In fact, the roots govern what shape the tree will grow. The trunk and branches are all determined by what roots are growing underneath.

The trunk of the tree reflects the roots in its height and strength. Some are large in diameter. Others, not so much. But each trunk is the source of strength for branches and, ultimately, the fruit at the end of those branches. It symbolizes our performance. It's visible and eventually leads to our outcomes.

Ultimately, the branches and fruit reveal the type of tree. An apple tree or an orange tree can be identified by the small red or orange produce springing from its branches. In fact, the fruit is what substantiates that the tree is actually valuable. It's the crop. It's why you plant those trees. As musician Bob Marley wrote, "When the root is strong, the fruit is sweet."

WHO BEFORE WHAT

It's no coincidence Jesus chose to use the metaphor of a tree when he spoke of our behavior—saying that we "know the tree by its fruit." A good tree cannot bear bad fruit, and a bad tree cannot bear good fruit (Luke 6:43). What determines that fruit, however, are its seeds and roots. Show me the root, and I can tell you the fruit. Check out the diagram below:

OUTCOME

PERFORMANCE

IDENTITY

This diagram is a reminder that leaders are foolish to answer the "what" question, unless they've first answered the "who" question. "What do you want to do?" is about trunks and branches, but that question is secondary. "Who are you?" is the root question and always determines everything else. The root is where it all begins.

A college student I supervised came close to a nervous breakdown. So full of angst, Cory finally caved and saw a counselor. In their meeting, he described how busy he was with a full load of classes, two part-time jobs, and a fraternity house full of expectations. No one on campus was busier than Cory. After listening to him groan about his life, the therapist diagnosed his problem. "I know what your problem is," Cory's therapist said. "You've become a 'human-doing' before you've ever let yourself become a 'human-being.'"

Wow, was she right.

Cory felt like he could fill his life with activities, answering the "what" question with a truckload of busyness and good endeavors. Sadly, it was the only question he'd asked himself. His wise counselor forced him to answer the "who" question: Who are you?

Too many of us who serve our Savior jumped right into the "what" and got busy. Oh, boy did we get busy. After all, our organizations want results, right? Eventually, we burn out because we didn't resolve the "who" question first. It's like attaching "artificial fruit" to the branches. It may appear authentic, but its not—it is plastic and contrived (and it doesn't taste good either).

INCARNATIONAL LEADERSHIP

During my years with John Maxwell, we discussed the diagram below several times. We referred to it as the "Incarnational Leadership" columns. Check it out:

WHO I AM? (MY BEING)	WHAT I DO? (MY BEHAVIOR)	THE RESULT? (MY OUTCOME)
1. A visionary leader	1. Set goals for the team	1. High morale on the team
2. A humble leader	2. Depend on God	2. God's power on me
3. A leader with integrity	3. Do what is right, ethical	3. Trust and momentum

The key to making the columns work efficiently is to address them from left to right—to work on our "being" and answer the "who" questions first. Our problem is that we seldom approach it this way. We are so production oriented that we leap over to the right-hand column and ask, "How do I gain high morale on my team? How do I get loyal team members? How do I earn the people's trust and gain momentum?"

We do this too often in America because we value results and productivity. We tend to focus immediately on the product instead of the process.

We'll take any fruit… even if it's artificial.

If we begin with results and outcomes and move in the wrong direction, we will be forced to conjure up all the right behaviors in that middle column, grunting and striving to set goals artificially instead depending on God and having those aspirations grow up from our identity in Him (our natural roots). Do you know how challenging this is? It's actually impossible to do this over the long haul with mere human effort. So, what does God do?

God gently nudges us to start from left to right. Begin with "who I am." Then, we naturally bear fruit. Real fruit always comes from the right root. For example, look at number one: If I am a visionary leader…I will naturally set goals. (It's what visionaries naturally tend to do). Ultimately, I will naturally experience high morale on my team. The left-hand column is the root. The middle column is the trunk. The right-hand column is the fruit

God works miracles when we get the order right. He grows leaders from the inside out. Fruit is a natural outcome of a healthy identity. Effective leaders always lead this way. Stephen Covey wrote, "You can't change the fruit without changing the root."[3]

What's in the Way?

Even smart people struggle with this. In the 19th century, Ralph Waldo Emerson told Henry David Thoreau, "At Harvard they teach all branches of learning." Thoreau replied, "Yes, but they don't teach the roots."

So what are the root issues of this identity thing?

1. **Awareness**—Knowing my identity. I must be aware of my gift-mix: my personal talents, acquired skills, traits, and personality that make me unique.

2. **Affirmation**—Hearing those I respect affirm my value. Then, I must learn to affirm myself and recognize my own value.

3. **Association**—Participating in a community where it is safe to make mistakes. Then, I must be accountable and supportive of others as I belong.

4. **Achievement**—Facing challenges and using my strengths. I must find ways to add value to others through those gifts.

The truth is, most of us don't stop to ask the "who" question, or if we do, we don't like the answer. It isn't flashy enough, so we pretend to be like someone else, and don't become the best version of ourselves. Actor Sean Connery was once asked why he kept acting, even though he's got plenty of money. His response? "Because I get the opportunity to be somebody better and more interesting than I am."

I wonder how many of us are acting and might confess to the same thing.

Early in my career, I served under a supervisor who struggled with this truth. He acknowledged to me that the board of elders and the congregation intimidated him. He even told me he felt threatened by me. He was full of insecurities. Sadly, I watched the implications of his emotional deficits over the next two years. The church almost fell apart and he was fired from his position. He had strong gifts, but not strong roots.

Leadership professor Warren Bennis said it best when he said, "Becoming a leader is synonymous with becoming yourself. It is precisely that simple and it is also that difficult."[4]

LOOK AT THE BOOK: REFLECT AND RESPOND

1. Read Isaiah 37:31. *"Once more, a remnant of the kingdom of Judah will take root below and bear fruit above."* Note that God even works with nations in this way. Why is it challenging for us to focus on the root first?

   _____

   _____

2. Romans 12:2 reminds us that we are transformed by the "renewing of our minds." Paraphrase this verse in light of our predisposition to change from the outside in:

   _____

   _____

3. Read Proverbs 4:23 and II Corinthians 5:17. How is "inside out" identity reinforced?

   _____

   _____

ASSESS YOURSELF

As you reflect on your identity, indicate which of the areas below you've wrestled with as a person and leader. A healthy sense of identity includes four elements:

IDENTITY ELEMENT:	IF MISSING, I FEEL:	DO YOU STRUGGLE?
1. A sense of worth	1. Inferior	_____
2. A sense of belonging	2. Insecure	_____
3. A sense of competence	3. Inadequate	_____
4. A sense of purpose	4. Insignificant	_____

Rate Yourself: Which of these four elements do you struggle with the most?

TRY IT OUT: PRACTICING THE TRUTH

This week, find ways to practice the four elements of healthy identity roots:

  1. AWARENESS—Knowing my position in Christ and my personal strengths.

  How can you practice this?

2. **AFFIRMATION**—Hearing others affirm my value and affirming my own value.

How can you practice this?

3. **ASSOCIATION**—Participating in a community that operates like family.

How can you practice this?

4. **ACHIEVEMENT**—Facing challenges and adding value with my God-given gifts.

How can you practice this?

Surgeons and Vampires

THERE IS A RIGHT AND WRONG WAY TO OFFER FEEDBACK OR CRITICISM TO PEOPLE. VAMPIRES SUCK THE LIFEBLOOD RIGHT OUT OF A PERSON, OPERATING FROM THEIR OWN NEED. SURGEONS TAKE BLOOD TO TREAT MEDICAL CONDITIONS CAREFULLY AND CONSTRUCTIVELY. THOUGH BOTH DRAW BLOOD, THEY LEAD TO COMPLETELY DIFFERENT OUTCOMES.

I'm sure you've noticed the major comeback vampires have made in the media over the last twenty years. TV shows and movies have included several of those mythical parasites preying on their unsuspecting victims. For some reason, people seem to be entertained by it all. Vampires have been popular since the silent film era, long before Buffy was around to slay them.

At the same time, shows about doctors or surgeons have also been popular. I can't remember a time when there wasn't a drama about hospitals and medical professionals on TV. I wonder if our culture's fascination with both vampires and physicians illustrates that people are strangely drawn to stories that involve blood? And that curious fascination is a good starting point for this *Habitude*.

Blood has always symbolized life. We even see this idea in the term "lifeblood." Physiologically, we know that blood circulates through our bodies, enabling us to function, to breathe, to live.

This allows for an instructive comparison and contrast between vampires and surgeons. Have you ever taken a moment to consider that both draw blood when they perform? Both can be sources of pain, both break the skin, and both usually elicit stress for anyone who encounters them. Why? Because, no matter which one you run into, you are going to lose some blood. Beyond the blood loss, however, there is a huge difference between the surgeon and vampire.

OFFERING FEEDBACK TO OTHERS

The work of a vampire has a consequence. The work of a doctor leads to a benefit. Traditionally, vampires prey on unsuspecting victims, biting them on the neck with their fangs. In folklore, vampires are defined by their need to feed on blood and are driven by their manipulative nature. This theme has remained common throughout the many film adaptations over the last century. A surgeon, on the other hand, carefully selects where the incision will go. The operation is done prudently and meticulously, cautiously treating a specific condition and sewing the skin back together so healing can result. With surgeons, the pain leads to gain.

My friend Brett Trapp first brought this idea to my attention. Poor leaders offer feedback a little bit like a vampire. Life-giving leaders do so like a surgeon, even when the feedback is critical and corrective. They draw blood so that life and health can be restored to their team members. One takes life. The other gives life.

How do you offer feedback to your team? Like a vampire or a surgeon?

Leading in High Stress Situations

We live in a day of elevated stress levels. Whether it's a school campus, a sports team, or a workplace, the stakes feel high, and just being on a team can often raise our anxiety. Because the competition is fierce, teams are constantly under pressure to improve or get left in the dust. This can lead to impatience, frustration, poor communication, and angst.

According to Robert Leahy, Director of the American Institute of Cognitive Therapy, the average teen today has the same anxiety level as the average psychiatric patient did in the 1950s. The level of stress we feel can foster "vampire style" leadership. Not only that, I often meet adults who are irritated at students and dissatisfied with their output. They claim young leaders don't display resilience; they act entitled, don't follow through on commitments, and are frequently just plain lazy. Of course, any of these realities are likely to create "high-stress interactions," but in the midst of these very interactions, we have two choices of how to respond.

There are two common scenarios that surface in stressful contexts:

1. Most tend to lead out of **relief**.
2. The successful tend to lead out of *belief*.

The Motivation of Relief

Leading out of relief is what a "vampire" leader does. The goal is to satisfy an appetite or relieve stress. Parents do this when their kids exhaust them. Employers do this when they vent at young staffers who don't perform. You might be tempted to do this when you are feeling the pressure of school, work, or everyday life. You may simply feel overwhelmed. In these moments, we often want to relieve the current negative emotions we feel.

Sadly, while relief is the quicker and easier option, it is not the long-term solution. Just like a vampire, this type of leadership aims to quickly satisfy a pressing appetite.

We tend to be motivated by relieving the pain rather than believing in the person. It's usually one or the other—relief or belief.

Relief is our natural default style of leadership. When facing a difficult situation, we seek to ease the pain, to get a quick fix for ourselves and for those that we lead. Our goal is to relieve the tension. The point is that without intention, we can all be natural vampires.

At times, it's about our relief. We choose the easy route and appease others, giving in to their requests. It makes life easier, at least in the moment. And sometimes, we lead out of relief by venting our anger. Sadly, anger is punitive rather than redemptive.

And sometimes, it's about their relief. We want to relieve others of the consequences that come with poor choices or behaviors because they're so stressed out. As you know, students have so many pressures on them with grades, sports, and standardized tests. When you empathize with others' situations, it feels right to let them off the hook. And while it does ease their pain temporarily, it doesn't empower those under your leadership to grow and improve. Sadly, this approach is permissive rather than redemptive.

In short, venting feels good to me and lets me off hook. Caving feels good to them and lets them off the hook. Both reactions compromise good leadership. I'm like a vampire.

THE MOTIVATION OF BELIEF

In a challenging situation, "surgeon" leaders operate out of fundamental belief in the potential of those they lead. We pull out the best in them when we believe the best about them. Research from psychologist, Diana Baumrind, from U.C. Berkeley reminds us that people are most productive when we are both responsive and demanding.

1. RESPONSIVE TO THEM—We are attentive, supportive, and caring. We love, understand, and believe in them.

2. DEMANDING OF THEM—Because we believe in them, we cannot allow them settle for less than their best. We hold them to high standards.[5]

This is what every human being needs. As you seek to become a life-giving leader, one of the most important skills to master is knowing when to be responsive to the needs of those you lead and when to demand the best out of them.

Often, we must do both at the same time.

Daniel Coyle and a team of psychologists from Stanford, Yale and Columbia explored the concept of feedback and which type received the best results.[6] They asked middle school teachers to give a writing project to their students and afterward, offer them various types of responses. To their surprise, the researchers discovered there was one particular approach to criticism that improved effort so much they labeled it "magical." Students who received this feedback chose to revise their papers far more often than students who did not—a 40 percent increase among white students and a 320 percent boost among black students.[7] In the end, it improved performances significantly. The approach to criticism was rather simple. Teachers explained that they had high expectations of their students: *"I'M GIVING YOU THESE COMMENTS BECAUSE I HAVE HIGH EXPECTATIONS OF YOU AND I KNOW YOU CAN REACH THEM."*

Of course, the words are not magic, but the thought behind them is profound. They communicated the challenge from a fundamental belief in their students. You and I can adopt this type of life-giving leadership as well, but it will require tough love with patience and tenacity to follow through. It's effective when our leadership stems from a deep-seated belief in those we are leading.

I once heard a story about an important figure in American history that—whether it is urban legend or fact—continues to inspire me as a teacher and leader. Thomas Edison is said to have shared the circumstances of how he became such an incredible inventor. When young Tom returned home from school one day, his mother noticed he had a piece of paper in his hand. It was a note from his teacher, and his mom was the only one who was supposed to read it. When she did, she grew tearful. Predictably, the boy asked what it said.

His mother paused, then replied, "Your son is a genius. This school is too small for him and doesn't have enough good teachers to train him. Please teach him yourself."

From then on, Edison's mom removed him from school, and he was self-taught. She allowed him to curiously pursue what interested him and to devour it.

Years later, after his mom died, Edison was rummaging through her belongings and came across that note from his teacher. When he read it, he was stunned. It read, "Your son is addled (mentally ill). We won't let him come to school anymore. We don't have the teachers to handle him. You'll have to teach him yourself."

Edison wept for hours and since that time, gave his mother credit for cultivating his genius as an inventor. She saw something in her son that others didn't. What she read to him and what that note actually said ultimately led to the same result: Tom had to learn at home. But, the belief behind that circumstance meant everything to him.

Someone had chosen to believe in him.

1. Colossians 4:6 tells us that our conversation should always be full of grace, our words "seasoned with salt," so we can appropriately respond to each person.

_____

_____

2. Why is it leaders get anxious and often lead like vampires instead of surgeons?

_____

_____

3. What prevents us from seeing the potential in someone and believing in them?

_____

_____

4. Proverbs 18:21 says, "Death and life are in the power of the tongue." Paraphrase this verse in light of the surgeon and the vampire.

_____

_____

ASSESS YOURSELF

After reviewing the two columns, mark an X on the line that accurately describes you:

WHEN I AM A VAMPIRE	WHEN I AM A SURGEON
1. I am thinking about me	1. I am thinking about you
2. I may use sarcasm or hyperbole	2. I will be careful and accurate
3. I surprise the person as I attack	3. I carefully plan our encounter
4. I look backward at a past flaw	4. I look forward to future possibilities
5. I may assault the person's character	5. I cautiously remove the problem
6. Short-term gain; long-term pain	6. Short term-pain; long-term gain

In times of crisis, would those around you describe you as more of a surgeon or vampire? Be honest as you place an X on the spectrum below.

VAMPIRE --- SURGEON

Try it Out: Practicing the Truth

When we lead out of "belief" we produce superior results. Next week, attempt to prepare for every discussion you have with those you are leading by asking yourself the following questions:

- What must be said or done to display my belief in them?

- How would I handle a less-than-optimal performance if I genuinely believed they could perform better?

- How would my words change?

Keep a log of how your conversations and results change over seven days. Talk about it with other leaders. What happened?

Practice Coach

HEAD BASKETBALL COACH OF THE UNIVERSITY OF CALIFORNIA AT LOS ANGELES JOHN WOODEN WAS CALLED A "PRACTICE COACH." HE PREPARED HIS PLAYERS TO HEAR HIS VOICE DURING GAMES BY ROLLING UP A PROGRAM AND TALKING THROUGH IT AT PRACTICE. DURING GAMES, THEY COULD DISTINGUISH HIS VOICE FROM THE CROWD. SPIRITUAL LEADERS DO THE SAME WITH GOD.

Coach John Wooden is a hero of mine. Yep, me and millions of other basketball fans. The media called him "the Wizard of Westwood" because he had coached his teams to ten national championships, but he actually referred to himself as an educator. For him, the game of basketball was just a vehicle to teach his student athletes about life.

THE WIZARD OF WESTWOOD

His former players stayed in touch with him long after graduation. Kareem Abdul-Jabbar, who played at UCLA, later wrote, "Coach Wooden had a profound influence on me as an athlete, but an even greater influence on me as a human being. He is responsible, in part, for the person I am today." Bill Walton astutely observed that and said, "We have become John Wooden ourselves." In one sense, they did so by embracing Wooden's beliefs, character, and values as their own.

John Wooden was known as a "practice coach." He focused on the process rather than the game. He understood that if his players embraced the process of preparation correctly, the games would take care of themselves. So, he taught them everything from how to put their socks on correctly (to avoid blisters) to the expectations for conduct before and after a game. But there is one element of his instruction that stands out for me that I'd like to focus on: he taught his players to listen to him.

Wooden was known for rolling up a program and holding it to his mouth during games. He could communicate with his team this way amidst the noise of the crowd. It was a sort of megaphone. What I love about this man, however, is that he knew he had to condition them to distinguish his voice from others, so he actually rolled up the program during practice and spoke to his players, just like he would in a game.

At times, he was known to bring in other UCLA students to simulate noise in the gym. They were asked to yell and scream at the players as loud as possible. Then, in the midst of that noise, Wooden would roll up his program and direct his players. And this teaching strategy worked. They could hear him and follow his direction in the worst of noisy arenas. His teams went on to win more championships than any other NCAA basketball team in history.

I love the picture this paints of spiritual leadership.

Our Number One Job as Leaders

You see, the primary task of spiritual leadership is attentiveness to God. Ministry begins in God. It continues in God. It ends in God. Staying focused on him is the central challenge of ministry. I must understand that I can lead others to recognize God's presence in their world only when I am first aware of God's presence in my own world. So, my questions are as follows:

- How consciously aware are you of God's presence in your leadership?
- Have you learned to listen and to hear his voice amidst the noise?
- Are you first listening before you're leading anyone?
- Are you practicing his presence as you serve and lead?

Good leaders are ultimately good followers—hearing God's voice and obeying him, regardless of the crowd and clutter around them. Like the UCLA Bruins listening to Wooden, we must learn to separate God's voice from the noise.

The Question of Ownership

In many ways, this is not only about hearing God's voice, it's a question of ownership. As we do work, do we assume ownership of the ministry, or do we keep it where it belongs—in the hands of God. Do we play the role of COO, and let God remain the CEO, or do we subtly begin to take control again when we finish our opening prayer and the work begins?

When I was young, our family had a dog named Pepper. He was a large, black poodle who was as sanguine as a dog could be. He loved going outside to play, run, explore, and meet anyone who had time for him. I noticed over time that Pepper learned to tune in to my voice. In fact, he was intimately acquainted with the voices of each of our family members: my dad, my mom, my sisters, and me. As he romped around outside, regardless of who was around him, he could always distinguish our voice over the others, and he'd quickly come if we beckoned him. It was quite astonishing.

In short, Pepper knew his owners. And even though he created quite an agenda for himself when he went outside, our voice always trumped his agenda. Why? Because we were not just his friends, we owned him. When we called, he'd stop and come to us.

What a great picture for us as spiritual leaders. Dallas Willard once said, "Our failure to hear God's voice when we want to is due to the fact that, in general, we do not want to hear it; that we only want to hear it when we think we need it."

As leaders, we'll hear his voice consistently when we acknowledge that God is our owner and not our servant.

Learning to Hear His Voice

It is a fundamental and daily practice for me to remember that my primary job as a spiritual leader is to mind God and to hear his voice. Period.

Jesus modeled this as he healed a crowd of people in Simon Peter's home (Mark 1). Before he finished meeting everyone's needs, he left Simon's house and went out to pray. Then, he moved on. Although there were still unmet needs, he spent time with God first to receive fresh direction. The goal wasn't merely about meeting every need; it was about doing his father's bidding.

Insights on Hearing God's Voice in Our Leadership

1. God's word is described in scripture as both "logos" and "rhema." It is both timeless and timely. Logos describes his word to everyone, as revealed in the Bible. Rhema describes a timely word, spoken for the moment. Nehemiah, for instance, was well acquainted with the written Word of God but heard God beckon him to build a wall. That particular word was for Nehemiah in that moment of time, not for everyone else.

2. God's inward promptings (rhema) are always aligned with scripture (logos) and with God's nature, which is revealed in the scripture. In other words, he won't prompt us to do anything contrary to what he does or says in the logos. Jesus was the Word made flesh who visited us in history but was revealed through prophetic scripture.

3. God's inward promptings will feel better than our own thoughts or ideas, as if they're coming from another source... because they are. Young Samuel heard God's voice in the night and thought it was Eli's. You'll sense that God's prompting is superior to yours. In Isaiah 55:8, God said, "My thoughts are not your thoughts."

4. God's inward promptings may be frightening but are generally accompanied by an inward peace. Colossians 3:15 instructs us to let God's peace "umpire" in our hearts. Although his direction may be counterintuitive—like marching around Jericho— you'll sense it is right, and you somehow feel peaceful about doing his bidding.

5. The quicker you obey God's promptings, the clearer they become. The more you hesitate, the fuzzier they become. I have discovered this over time. If I am not committed to do what he says, he may stop revealing insights. The key is to be willing to take a risk and obey. Confirmation comes along the way, as shown in John 7:17.

6. The purpose of his promptings are to edify, direct, confirm, or encourage a person who needs to trust him more deeply. We don't hear his voice to brag about it or to get goose bumps. Consider Moses at the burning bush or Saul heading to Damascus. He speaks to offer peace, purpose, or a path to make progress toward a goal.

THE ADVENTURE OF TUNING IN

A few months ago, I visited my bank to transfer some money to another account. It was a busy day for me, so the last thing on my mind was spending time at the bank. As I sat down with an account manager, however, I heard God's gentle whisper (I Kings 19:12) prompt me to ask her about her father. Weird. I didn't even know her, nor if her dad was even alive. But, I did know it was God's prompting. So, as she typed on the keyboard, I quietly asked, "How's your dad doing?"

She stopped abruptly and looked me straight in the eye. "How did you know?"

I smiled and said, "I don't know anything, except that I wanted to ask about your dad." It was then she revealed her father had just been taken to the hospital in Russia. He'd had a heart attack, and she'd be on the next flight out to visit him that night. This opened up an incredible conversation. I explained that I felt God prompting me to ask her about him and to pray for her. She cried as I got to minister to her in that most unlikely context. It all started with a prompting from him.

Living and leading while listening to God opens life into an absolute adventure. It enables us to be countercultural and offers peace, even when everyone else may be filled with angst.

I have a friend who moved to Milwaukee in 1982. One Saturday, his Wisconsin Badgers were playing football and getting beaten badly. He said it was gruesome to sit in the stands and watch them get whipped that day.

But, something strange was happening in the crowd. At random times during the game, thousands of fans would spontaneously cheer. It obviously had nothing to do with the game. So, what was it? My friend inquired about the cheering and the guy next to him simply said, "Oh, all of us who just shouted—we're listening on our radios to the Brewers. Our baseball team is in the World Series for the first time, and we just scored against the Cardinals."

Suddenly, it made sense. As they watched a game in the stands, they tuned in to a different broadcast full of good news. They were listening to another voice.

I trust that if we are tuned into God's frequency, that could be our story as well. After all, God has his program rolled up and ready.

Look at the Book: Reflect and Respond

1. Examine Isaiah 30:21. "Whether you turn to the right or to the left, your ears will hear a voice behind you, saying, "This is the way; walk in it." When have you felt you have heard God's voice? How does he prompt you?

   _____

   _____

2. Jesus said, "I am the Good Shepherd. I know my sheep, and my sheep know me... My sheep listen to my voice." (John 10:14, 27). How did you learn to hear his voice?

   _____

   _____

3. In Daniel 1:8-21, we see three characteristics of Daniel and his friends: resolve, respect, and receptivity. How did hearing from God earn Daniel influence?

   _____

   _____

Assess Yourself

Reflect on your leadership. Mark an X at the spot on the line that accurately describes you:

1. I find it easy to slow down and listen for God's promptings amidst the noise:

   No -- Yes

2. My life and calendar are so full, but I carve out time daily to spend with God:

   No -- Yes

3. I practice the presence of God in my weekly routines:

   No -- Yes

Try it Out: Practicing the Truth

This week, review the list of six insights above on hearing God's voice. Practice his presence, and when you sense a prompting, obey it. If it aligns with scripture, take a risk and initiate. Follow through and see what happens. Next week, report back to your community how things went. Are you hearing his voice more clearly?

Clean Windows

IS THE WORD "CLEAN" A VERB OR AN ADJECTIVE? IS IT AN ACTION OR A GOAL? DO YOU WANT YOUR TEAM TO "CLEAN THE WINDOWS" OR DO YOU WANT "CLEAN WINDOWS" AS AN END GOAL? EFFECTIVE LEADERS COMMUNICATE CLEAR OUTCOMES. THEY ARE DESCRIPTIVE RATHER THAN PRESCRIPTIVE IN THEIR VISION.

Every leader has struggled with good people who misinterpret their direction or vision. Often, leaders give instructions only to have team members disappoint them in their execution of those orders. Consider this scenario: When you ask someone to "wipe down the windows," they will wipe them down. The window may end up with streaks all over it or smudges in certain places, but the person gave you exactly what you asked for—they wiped the windows down. If instead, you ask a team member to "make the window crystal clear," they will deliver what you asked for—a beautiful "crystal clear" window.

However, if the objective is clear enough, how they clean that window should be up to them.

MANAGEMENT BY OBJECTIVE

The key to having "clean windows" is to manage by objective. Instead of telling people what to do, lasting leaders describe the outcome they hope for and allow the person to surprise them with their innovation. This requires our leadership to be "descriptive" not "prescriptive." We must stop prescribing every step along the way, as if we were doing the task. Instead, we should describe the result we want and let those great team members demonstrate what they can do. This allows them to put on display the gifts, creativity, and energy they possess by owning how they reach the goal.

There are, of course, some inexperienced team members that will need leaders to be prescriptive in their instruction. In those cases, leaders must suggest particular steps they should take. Most of the time, however, we leaders tend to micromanage and require team members to pursue goals in the exact same manner we would ourselves. The result is that team members often don't "own" the goal. They are simply trudging through a task we own that they are merely renting from us.

"Management by objective" occurs when a leader describes an outcome they want to see happen—an objective they desire accomplished—and they turn a team member loose to go after it in their own way. The benefits of this style of leadership are many:

- THE TEAM MEMBERS GET TO USE THEIR CREATIVITY AND GIFTS.

- THE TEAM MEMBERS BEGIN TO "OWN" THE PROJECT.

- THE TEAM MEMBERS LIKELY ACHIEVE THE GOAL FASTER DOING IT THEIR WAY.

- THE TEAM MEMBERS INVEST MORE ENERGY BECAUSE THEY CHOSE THE METHOD.

From the beginning of our organization—Growing Leaders—I knew my best style of leadership for both interns and our young team members was "management by objective." In fact, I prefer hiring college upperclassmen or recent graduates instead of freshmen as interns simply because they're often more mature and ready for the ownership necessary under this kind of leadership style.

SITUATIONAL LEADERSHIP

Years, ago, authors Ken Blanchard and Paul Hersey coined the term "situational leadership."[8] It's a model explaining that people respond better to various kinds of leadership, based on their experience and maturity. While the theory was developed in the 1970s, it has evolved over time. Here are the four styles:

Style 1—Telling
This is a more directive style, characterized by one-way instruction, defining the role of the person and providing the what, how, when, and where of the task at hand.

Style 2—Selling
This is a more interactive style, using two-way conversation to define the task and providing support that allows the person to buy into the project.

Style 3—Participating
This is a more relational style, issuing fewer task behaviors and engaging both the leader and the person to determine how the job will be done.

Style 4—Delegating
This style is empowering, as it relays the outcome you desire but leaves the methods and responsibility to the individual. The leader is only a monitor.

Over time, leaders should consistently cast the vision, define the culture, and embody the values so they can move toward Style 3 and Style 4 with their team members. When team members constantly see excellence modeled by leaders and hear it communicated as a goal, they're more apt to display it themselves. We must help them to see what we see, love what we love, and desire what we desire.

Antoine de Saint-Exupery once said, "If you want to build a ship, don't herd people together to collect wood and don't assign them tasks and work, but rather, teach them to long for the endless immensity of the sea."

What This Looks Like in Real Life

Years ago, an executive at the Six Flags Over Georgia theme park heard that his custodial staff was providing horrible customer service at their amusement park. Guests were complaining about their attitudes and tempers. So, the executive did something interesting: he dressed up like a custodian and joined the staff for a day.

No one recognized him, and he could discover what was going on, incognito. After just one day on the job, the executive understood the problem. The custodians had merely been following the steps they'd been given. They believed their job was to keep the park clean. Since the patrons always messed it up, they quickly became the enemy. Custodians, in turn, became adversarial toward those customers. The result, of course, was that everyone was resentful.

Once back in his office, the executive did some re-training with the staff. He taught them that the ultimate goal was to please the customers. Period. Now, obviously, those customers enjoy a clean park, but that was secondary. Soon, their service improved measurably. They saw the big picture and began to "own" the executive's vision.

You might say, that executive shifted from saying "clean the windows" to saying, "Do whatever you must to make sure the windows are crystal clear at all times."

For leaders, the shift must be to:

- Focus on "outcomes" (ultimate goals) rather than "inputs" (specific tasks).
- Focus on scoring accomplishments, not merely doing activities.
- Focus on teaching them how to think, not just what to think.
- Focus on describing a goal, not prescribing a behavioral role.

"Make sure all the windows in the front of our store are crystal clear at all times," is a much better goal than telling employees to "wipe down the windows when you get a chance." The second statement is plain and simple but does not expect much from the recipient. They are merely following orders. They might even do the bare minimum. The first directive above expects excellence and clearly states the desired outcome, while also leaving the execution of the task up to the person to whom it is assigned. They become "owners" of both the vision and the task.

It is unwise to expect someone to be the owner and leader when you have only asked for them to be a follower.

Years ago, I accidentally discovered this reality.

I was mentoring a community of university students when one of them sent me an email asking who was choosing the topic for the next week's session. I was teaching leadership strategies to this group, and up until then, I had facilitated each lesson as their instructor. After all, that's my job. When I saw the inquiry, I grabbed my laptop and typed in my response: "I can do that."

Or, at least that's what I meant to say.

Without knowing it, however, I had mistyped: the letter "i" on my keyboard is right next to the letter "u." Unwittingly, I sent the message back: "u can do that."

And he believed me.

At our next meeting, the students showed up ready to go. Before I could interrupt them, they proceeded to facilitate the discussion, the experiments, the learning and the outcomes. They were brilliant. In fact, they didn't even need me. I had never felt such satisfaction than in that meeting when my "mentees" taught themselves. They felt empowered because I sent the message, "u can do that."

I never told them it was an accident on my part.

When we set expectations (high or low), people usually perform to them. It all begins with the vision we cast and the way we ask them to engage. In the end, "clean windows" should always be a description (of their work's outcome) not a direction (of the task they're supposed to do). It should be an outcome, not an input. It's a very average piece of instruction but an excellent point of description of a job well done. Activity does not equal accomplishment.

Two out of three people are visual learners, so when given a vision of a preferred future, they will perform better than when given mere steps to follow. A vision allows their imagination to take over, spurring them on to results they never thought possible. It just takes a leader with the courage to cast a vision and turn them loose.

Now, let's go find out how clean those windows can actually be.

LOOK AT THE BOOK: REFLECT AND RESPOND

1. In Genesis God challenges Abraham to go to a place He will show him later. He goes without knowing the details of the journey yet. However, in Genesis 22:17 God does share the outcome: *"I will make your descendants like the stars of the sky and the sand on the seashore..."* Talk about how God was practicing "clean windows" with the Father of the Hebrews.

_____

_____

2. Why do so many leaders lead with specific steps rather than with vision? Why is there a tendency to just say, "Clean the windows?"

_____

_____

3. In John 4:10, Jesus reminds the woman at the well that she had not caught the big idea she needed to embrace. He said, _"If you knew the gift of God and who it is that asks you for a drink, you wold have asked him and he would have given you living water."_ How was He practicing "clean windows" with her?

_____

_____

4. Why do so many team members fail to catch a vision for excellence from their leader?

_____

_____

5. How have you been led in the past? When you were new on the job, did you have supervisors who merely said, "Clean the windows," or did you have one who offered you a vision?

_____

_____

Assess Yourself

Reflect on your leadership. Mark an X at the point on the line that accurately describes you:

1. I find myself naturally leading others by describing detailed steps for completing tasks.
   FALSE --- TRUE

2. I tend to micromanage team members because they often don't see the big picture.
   FALSE --- TRUE

3. I'm not good at trusting others with a task that I delegate.

   FALSE -- TRUE

4. I find it difficult to cast a vision for an excellent outcome.

   FALSE -- TRUE

TRY IT OUT: PRACTICING THE TRUTH

This week, I'd like to suggest a game plan for your leadership: List a handful of important projects that someone on your team could accomplish if you delegated that project well. Next, write out a clear description of how the task would look if done with excellence—jot down your vision for the project if you were putting your best effort into it. Then, take that "vision" as an outcome (clean windows), meet with an appropriately gifted team member, and use that as a guide in your delegation. If they need suggestions on steps to take, go ahead and offer them, but only if they ask. When these projects are finished, evaluate what happened.

Salutes and Snubs

IN THE MILITARY, THE HIGHEST FORM OF GREETING IS A SALUTE AND IS USUALLY RESERVED FOR OFFICERS. LIFE-GIVING LEADERS REMOVE THE RANKS OF TEAM MEMBERS AND TREAT EVERYONE, REGARDLESS OF STATUS, WITH COMPLETE RESPECT—SALUTING OTHERS AS OFFICERS INSTEAD OF SNUBBING THEM AS ROOKIES.

We've all seen military soldiers salute someone of a higher rank as they enter the room. In military traditions throughout history, there have been numerous methods of performing salutes: hand gestures, hoisting flags, or maybe removing headgear. The nature of the salute is the acknowledgement that someone deserving deference and honor has walked into your presence.

I will never forget, as a young boy, watching the funeral service for President John F. Kennedy on television. Soldiers from all branches of our military stopped to salute the casket of their former commander in chief before saluting the other officers present. It was an incredible display of respect and reverence. They conducted themselves as if they were in the presence of nobility.

There are two memorable accounts of the origin of our modern salute.

Some historians believe it dates back to European monarchies. When citizens saw their queen approaching, they would raise their hand just above their eyes, as if to shield their eyes from the bright glow of her face. Obviously, there was no real glow, but it was a gesture of honor. It was a visual response to the queen's "radiant beauty," which required those nearby to create shade above their eyes, just as we might do when looking into a sunny sky.

According to current military manuals, the modern Western salute originated when knights greeted each other. To signal friendly intentions, they would raise their visors to show their faces—a salute of sorts. Others also note that raising your visor was a way to identify yourself by saying, "This is who I am, and I'm not afraid."

In both cases, the salute was a sign of relationship and respect.

The person saluting was saying, "I acknowledge and honor you, and I am revealing my good intentions."

Today's Vanishing Salute

In our world today, displays of respect are diminishing. Our culture is far less formal than in the past. We wear casual clothes at work or while traveling more than we did a century ago, we use more familiar language—even with strangers—and we greet people with a more personal tone than salutations from the 19th and 20th centuries. In one sense, this can be seen as a step in the right direction. No one likes people who act stuffy. The Victorian Age is, indeed, a thing of the past.

Sadly, however, these casual displays do have a downside.

In most places, the natural respect we once demonstrated for the elderly or for authorities is in decline. In public transportation, we need signs to remind us to allow older or disabled people to have our seat on the train. We don't naturally practice respectful manners unless we've been taught to do so. When we talk to people, we seldom maintain good eye contact. In fact, we now hide behind technology to snub others. It happens all the time.

Focusing on your phone in a social setting is known as "phubbing"—which is a combination of "phone" and "snubbing." A relatively new study published in the journal *Computers in Human Behavior* examined what motivates people to "phub" and how it seems to have become a normal part of life. It's a lazy person's way of avoiding social contact. People will commonly just stare at their phone instead of acknowledging someone right next to them.[9]

Most of us have probably snubbed someone in our past. It is the opposite of respect. It means to pay no attention and to ignore the presence of someone, offering no acknowledgment, but treating them with contempt or neglect.

It is no coincidence that the words "snub" and "snob" are pronounced so similarly. If you've been on the other side of snubbing, you know it doesn't feel very good.

Snubbing is often the new normal. Friendships or dating relationships frequently end when someone simply stops texting or messaging the other. When we don't know how to have a hard conversation, we merely choose to have no conversation. We avoid. We ignore. We snub. It's socially easier than showing respect.

Great teams fight "snubbing" and find ways to "salute" each other.

Respect is a Choice

When I talk to college students, they usually explain their lack of respect toward professors, police, or politicians by saying those individuals have not earned their respect. They've acted in a way that doesn't deserve our esteem. Very often, I agree. However, I have come to believe that respect must be a choice. It's something we choose to give, not something we demand others to earn all the time. While I believe leaders should act in a respectful manner, our culture makes progress only when we determine to give respect as a rule, not an exception.

Respect should be given unconditionally.

When we do that, I believe respect breeds respect.

I vividly remember the 1968 presidential election between Richard Nixon and Hubert Humphrey. The Republican and Democrat candidates saw issues very differently but cultivated a friendship during their political careers. Despite their differences, they called and visited each other over the years—asking about each other's families, laughing at jokes, and talking about vacations. In 1972, when President Nixon was reelected, one of the first calls he got was from Humphrey congratulating him on his victory. What I remember most, however, was when Hubert Humphrey died in 1978. Photos from the funeral appeared on the news, and Richard Nixon—his political opponent—sat next to his Humphrey's wife, Muriel, during the memorial. Once again, it's a great picture of two leaders finding a way to salute each other.

THE PECKING ORDER

If you were to ask someone, "Who deserves respect?" they might commonly say it depends on one or all of three categories:

1. RESULTS—We feel if someone's talent produces results, they deserve respect.

2. RELATIONSHIP—We feel if someone is closely connected to us, they deserve respect.

3. RANK—We feel if someone has a higher spot in the flow chart, they deserve respect.

The "pecking order" is a widespread and common approach to respect. It is logical to most people, even if they fail to practice it. Unfortunately, this view often leads us to excuse ourselves from showing respect to those who don't qualify for it.

But, what if you lived differently? What if you did away with perceived rank and treated everyone like a VIP? What if everyone received the respect of an officer? What if the star player on the team and the last guy on the bench were both respected by the entire team? What if the celebration for winning included everyone equally?

Our research reveals these six results when that happens:

- MORALE GOES UP TANGIBLY
- ETHICS AND WORK ETHIC RISES
- CAMARADERIE INCREASES
- SACRIFICE ON BEHALF OF THE TEAM RISES
- COLLABORATION SKYROCKETS
- PRODUCTION EXPANDS AMONG THE TEAM

Where Respect Truly Begins

I believe I owe everyone a basic level of respect for being fellow human beings but realize that my level of respect will vary from person to person. We all know, by nature, that we tend to hold some people in higher regard for who they are and what they've done. But actually, our level of respect has less to do with who they are and more to do with who we are.

In short, respect begins with self-respect.

If I don't possess a level of self-respect, if I can't look in the mirror and genuinely admire the face staring back at me, my respect for others will diminish. At best, our show of respect will be artificial. I cannot give away what I don't have. We must respect ourselves before we can enjoy what I've described in this chapter. Laurence Stone summarized the role of each this way:

> *"RESPECT FOR OURSELVES GUIDES OUR MORALS;*
> *RESPECT FOR OTHERS GUIDES OUR MANNERS."[10]*

You likely remember NFL quarterback Colin Kaepernick who sat down on the bench instead of standing during the national anthem during the 2016—2017 football season. This led to a firestorm from angry fans who felt he was disrespecting the flag and the military. Colin was simply protesting social injustice and police brutality. This episode has bred further controversy, but it's the story behind Kaepernick's story that I appreciate most.

A former Army Green Beret named Nate Boyer wrote an open letter to Colin explaining how his actions felt disrespectful. Colin replied by saying he never meant to disrespect anyone, but he believed the freedom and equality the military fought for wasn't being honored for all Americans. This led to a great meeting where Colin and Nate listened to each other and spoke their minds. The result? Nate suggested Colin could still protest by taking a knee rather than sitting on the bench. Taking a knee is a common act a soldier might observe for a fallen brother, like flying a flag at half-staff. It means that a brother has died. This solution allowed both sides to feel they were respected, but it required two men with opposing views to salute each other.

Look at the Book: Reflect and Respond

1. In ancient Hebrew culture, men commonly viewed both Gentiles and females with less respect. Jesus, however, displayed respect for both with his time and attention. Give examples of how Jesus revolutionized our view of respect for others.

_____

_____

2. I Peter 2:17 tells us to, *"show proper respect to everyone, love the family of believers, fear God, honor the emperor."* Romans 12:10 raises the bar by challenging us to *"outdo yourselves in honoring one another."* How could you "outdo" each other in showing honor?

_____

_____

3. What are specific ways your team could "salute" each other and show respect?

_____

_____

4. What would your team look like if everyone gave and got respect from everyone?

_____

_____

ASSESS YOURSELF

Take a minute and think about how you give and receive respect. On a scale of one to ten (ten being the strongest), rate yourself in the following areas:

1. SELF RESPECT (I practice discipline in my physical, mental, and emotional health.)

   1   2   3   4   5   6   7   8   9   10

2. RESPECT FOR AUTHORITY (I consistently display honor to all in a role of authority.)

   1   2   3   4   5   6   7   8   9   10

3. RESPECT FOR TEAM (I demonstrate respect for all team members, no matter what.)

   1   2   3   4   5   6   7   8   9   10

4. RESPECT FOR EVERYONE (In general, I show respect to others as fellow humans.)

   1   2   3   4   5   6   7   8   9   10

Why did you give yourself the scores you did?

TRY IT OUT: PRACTICING THE TRUTH

Do some creative thinking. Identify one clear way you can communicate respect for yourself, your teammates or coworkers, your coaches or supervisors, and your fellow human beings.

Each display of respect may be unique, but practice them daily for one week. Ask someone to hold you accountable to follow through. Next, as a team, brainstorm some ways that everyone can "salute" each other and show respect. Afterwards, discuss the results. Did it raise morale? Did it feel fake? How could you make it a genuine habit for several weeks? How did your self-respect change by "saluting" others in your circle of influence? Talk about a customized salute for your team.

[Air Before Ground]

Air Before Ground

OUR MILITARY STRATEGICALLY PERFORMS ACCURATE AIR STRIKES, REMOVING ENEMY WEAPONS BEFORE FOOT SOLDIERS ADVANCE. THIS ACCELERATES THEIR RESULTS. SPIRITUAL LEADERS LAUNCH A PRAYER ATTACK BEFORE SERVING WITH BOOTS ON THE GROUND. KNEES COME BEFORE HANDS.

I will never forget the military campaign Americans have come to know as "Operation Desert Storm." I was thirty years old when it happened. Out of nowhere, the nation of Iraq invaded its small neighboring country, Kuwait. The Kuwaiti people were robbed, and the towns were pillaged as Iraqi soldiers violated their land.

When the United States decided to get involved, a strategy was laid out under General Norman Schwarzkopf. After diplomatic relations broke down with Iraq, we feared the Iraqi army would invade Saudi Arabia as well, so we laid out a three-stage plan:

- OPERATION DESERT SHIELD
- OPERATION DESERT STORM
- OPERATION DESERT FAREWELL

Desert Shield was all about protection. Schwarzkopf oversaw 750,000 troops in the Persian Gulf and Saudi Arabia to protect the area and inspect Iraqi ships moving in and out of the Persian Gulf.

Then, the real action began.

OPERATION DESERT STORM

Next, General Schwarzkopf planned and led Operation Desert Storm—an extended air campaign followed by a highly successful ground offensive—which defeated the Iraqi Army and liberated Kuwait in early 1991. The air attack was so overwhelming that reporters called it the "shock and awe" campaign. I watched our airstrikes on the news through the lens of the fighter pilot, and it felt a bit like viewing a video game on television. It was stunning.

This set the stage for phase two of Desert Storm.

Following five weeks of airstrikes, we sent in ground troops. This is when the war became almost unbelievable. On television, Americans began to watch one or two of our soldiers arrest hundreds of Iraqi soldiers. More than once, an entire Iraqi company of soldiers would climb from their bunker with their hands in the air in surrender to a relatively small band of allied troops. Amazingly, the ground war ended after a mere 100 hours of fighting. Later, it was actually called "The One Hundred Hour War."

The strategy was brilliant. The air attack of several weeks paved the way for a short and relatively simple victory on the ground. After it was over, Schwarzkopf was presented with military honors for leading this effective strategy.

A Picture for Us Today

I believe as we "wrestle" with principalities and powers in the spiritual realm, we must borrow a page from Norman Schwarzkopf's playbook. The strategy? An air attack should always precede a ground attack.

By this, I mean we must first wage war "in the air" through prayer before we move in "on the ground" with direct ministry to people. As the old saying goes, "We must talk to God about people before we talk to people about God."

I find it interesting that when the early Church first encountered challenges, the leaders saw how easy it would be to get distracted from the source of their strength. In essence, they said, "It is not right that we neglect the Word of God to wait tables." They then declared what they should do with their time, and number one of the list was to pray (Acts 6:4).

Lasting leaders realize it's not the cry of the people that determines their next move, but the calling of God. The early church leaders realized their first responsibility was to cover their work with intercession—to pray for the people they led.

In short, the primary job of the leader is to pray.

While this *Habitude* may sound obvious and unnecessary, it's essential for one huge reason: leaders usually are in charge because we have a "bias for action." Leaders are doers. We take initiative. We want to solve problems. We want to make things happen. We love and often live by Nike's mantra—just do it.

This makes pausing to pray first very challenging. It feels like an inaction.

A Case Study

We remember Nehemiah as a leader who rebuilt the walls around Jerusalem. When he took on that role, it was in response to a report about the tragic conditions of the ruined city. Do you recall what he did first, before he consulted the king, obtained the resources, rallied the workers and constructed the wall?

He prayed.

"Now it came about when I heard these words, I sat down and wept and mourned for days; and I was fasting and praying before the God of heaven." —Nehemiah 1:4

Although Nehemiah possessed a bias for action, he somehow knew his first action was not with his hands, but on his knees. It's always knees before hands. Look at the sequence of this leader's story. With each new step, he prioritized intercession:

- WHEN HE FOUND OUT ABOUT THE PROBLEM, HE PRAYED. (1:4)
- WHEN HE SPOKE TO THE KING ABOUT THE PROJECT, HE PRAYED. (2:4)
- WHEN ENEMIES CONFRONTED HIM AND HIS TEAM, HE PRAYED. (4:9)
- WHEN HE SIMPLY NEEDED GOD'S BLESSING ON HIS WORK, HE PRAYED. (5:19)
- WHEN HE WAS DESPERATE FOR STRENGTH, HE PRAYED. (6:9)
- WHEN HE WAS TEMPTED TO TAKE VENGEANCE ON HIS ENEMIES, HE PRAYED. (6:14)
- WHEN HE WAS STRUGGLING TO ENDURE, HE PRAYED. (13:14)
- WHEN HE NEEDED GOD'S MERCY AND FAITHFULNESS, HE PRAYED. (13:22, 29)

This man of action recognized he was over his head and must first engage these challenges on his knees. This is how we're designed to lead. Before Jesus changed the course of history on the cross, he first went to Gethsemane to pray. Perhaps author Wesley Deuwell best explained why this is so strategic for us when he said, "When men work, men work. But when men pray, God works."

How Do Leaders Pray?

Leaders know that prayer is not only our doorway to intimacy with God, but it is also our pathway to wage spiritual warfare. So, let's define prayer in military terms. When Schwarzkopf laid out his plan, it included three levels of implementation: logistical, tactical, and strategic. These identified the daily, mid-range and ultimate goals of the mission.

In the same way, I believe there are three levels of prayer. They describe the kinds of issues we pray about each week. I describe them below and offer an example of how we might pray each kind of prayer before a meeting or a service:

LOGISTICAL PRAYER—For the temporal things that revolve around me (Lord, bless me today. Help me to do well as I speak, help the microphones work, and help us to get done on time.)

TACTICAL PRAYER—For temporal things that serve the needs of others (Lord, bless the service today. May it inspire and enable people to reach th goals and experience joy and peace.)

STRATEGIC PRAYER—For the ultimate purposes of God (Lord, may you raise up disciples from this meeting. Even if the micropho don't cooperate, achieve your purpose and glorify your name.)

When I assess my prayer life, I find I often limit my prayers to the first tw categories. It's too easy to simply cover my meals, family blessings, and safe Leaders must pursue more than the first two. Prayer is about the rule and rei of God.

ARE YOU PRAYING FOR THE WATER OR THE WAR?

In II Kings 3, three kings set out to battle the Moabites. In route to win a w they ran out of water. Devastated, they wondered if God deserted them. Th found the prophet Elisha and begged him to pray for God to give them wat Elisha replied, "You shall not see wind nor shall you see rain; yet that valley sh be filled with water, so that you shall drink, both you and your cattle and yo beasts. But this is a slight thing in the sight of the Lord; He will also give t Moabites into your hand.

Do you see what Elisha was saying? In essence he said, "You sought the Lord, b you asked for the wrong thing. You prayed for the water not the war. You stopp seeking the ultimate goal when you feared your daily needs were in jeopardy. Ke your eye on the strategic, and he'll give you the logistical things you need." O lesson? Matthew 6:33—"Seek first the Kingdom of God and all these things w be added unto you."

I saw this first hand in 1990 when I was in a small plane crash in New Zealan After the crash, my body was dragged out of the airplane. I was conscious an immediately began praying. I was tempted to pray only for comfort as nurs bandaged my leg and head. Instead, I asked God to show me what he wante to achieve through this accident. He answered. In a few hours, folks from bo national television networks showed up to interview someone who'd seen th crash. They had no idea a crash survivor would be available. That evening, I g to share my faith in Jesus with three million New Zealanders on the 5, 6, and 1 p.m. news.

Leaders pray first. Leaders pray strategically, not just logistically. Why? The know that if their air attack is thorough, their ground attack will be accelerated

Check out Matthew 7:7-11. This famous passage on prayer outlines three types of prayer. Notice the types of prayer spiritual leaders can offer their ministries:

1. ASKING PRAYER—The prayer of faith
   When you know God's will and must claim it, laying hold of it by faith.

   _____

   _____

2. SEEKING PRAYER—The prayer of dedication
   When you don't know his will and must seek what it is and commit to it.

   _____

   _____

3. KNOCKING PRAYER—The prayer of intercession
   When you know his will, but must persist, since it's about someone else's will.

   _____

   _____

All three require a unique kind of tenacity. Can you list a personal example of each?

ASSESS YOURSELF

Reflect on your leadership. Mark an X at the spot on the line that accurately describes you:

1. LOGISTICAL PRAYER: I find myself naturally praying for today's temporal needs.
   No --- YES

2. TACTICAL PRAYER: I find myself praying for others, but usually for earthly blessings.
   No --- YES

3. STRATEGIC PRAYER: I find myself praying for God's ultimate vision of reconciliation.
   No --- YES

Try it Out: Practicing the Truth

This week, I'd like to suggest a game plan for your prayer life as a leader. Unless you have a stellar plan you don't want to change, try this biblical sequence of categories. For each category, you can list people or situations that fit:

1. Praise and Thanksgiving (Psalm 100:4)

   _____

   _____

2. Leaders and Authorities (I Timothy 2:1-2)

   _____

   _____

3. Local Community (Jeremiah 29:7)

   _____

   _____

4. Nations and Unreached People Groups (II Chronicles 7:14)

   _____

   _____

5. Laborers to be Sent to Outsiders (Matthew 9:36-38)

   _____

   _____

6. Needs and Concerns (I Peter 5:7)

   _____

   _____

Splashes and Waves

MANY LEADERS STEP ON THE PLATFORM AND SIMPLY MAKE A SPLASH, BUT ANYONE CAN DO THAT—NOTHING CHANGES. LIFE-GIVING LEADERS MAKE WAVES. THEIR WORK AND WORDS IGNITE MOVEMENTS THAT MOBILIZE TEAM MEMBERS TO BECOME THE BEST VERSIONS OF THEMSELVES.

I lived in San Diego, California, as a teen and through most of my early career. As you likely know, San Diego is a beautiful city with near perfect weather and is located next to the Pacific Ocean. Every summer the beaches and bays are full of swimmers, surfers, and sailors enjoying America's gigantic West Coast pool.

I recall the first time I visited the beach at ten years old. I was so excited to be at a Southern California beach that I ran into the water and began splashing everywhere and everyone. Excitement levels were high, and my self-awareness was low. I was completely unaware of how my splashes affected anyone around me. I was amused, while others became annoyed.

Suddenly, I noticed everyone looking out to the sea, their eyes growing bigger. When I finally turned to look for myself, it was too late. A mammoth wave came crashing in, knocking me over (along with anyone else who wasn't paying attention). I quickly learned that those ocean waves are powerful.

Obviously, I was powerless against that big wave. No matter how hard I tried that afternoon, I could not remain standing when a wave hit. The wave conquered me. I was a victim of its strength. I quickly discovered that all my splashing was nothing compared to the might of an incoming wave.

This illustration is also a picture of leadership. You see, there are two kinds of leaders: those who make splashes and those who make waves.

THE SPLASHERS

You've probably seen them both up front on a stage. The splashers are the ones who know some gimmicks and have some guts. They've got tricks up their sleeve, and their goal is to impress a crowd and entertain. They yearn for their audience to like them. They are so intent on this goal that they often go to extreme lengths to reach it—off the wall and on the edge techniques crafted to get the listeners to talk about them, tweet about them, blog about them, and take selfies with them. They won't admit it, but their secret ambition is to become Christian celebrities.

THE WAVE MAKERS

Leaders who make waves actually foster genuine life change. It isn't just about the momentary laughter at a conference or meeting; it's about moving people from one place to another. They catalyze permanent transformation by creating environments that equip people to actually live life differently. They're humble, authentic, life-giving leaders who want to call attention to others rather than themselves. They also understand that while "splashes" happen in a moment and cause excitement, waves build over time, starting small and becoming large in the end.

In short, leaders who make splashes are about momentary events and leaders who cause waves are about building a recurring process. A great event can happen overnight. A great process happens over time.

EVENTS AND PROCESS

Check out the two columns below. They summarize the role of both splashes and waves. We need both great events and great processes to follow those events to spark progress. An event can take place in a single day, but a process where true life change occurs happens over a period of weeks and months. Maybe years. Events are glitzy. Process is unglamorous. We need both, but far too often, we're good at hosting events but poor at creating a process.

THE EVENT	THE PROCESS
1. Motivates people	1. Matures people
2. Encourages decisions	2. Encourages development
3. Is a calendar issue	3. Is a consistency issue
4. Challenges people	4. Changes people
5. Usually about a big group	5. Usually about a small group
6. Is about information	6. Is about interaction
7. Becomes a catalyst	7. Becomes a culture
8. Easy to pull off	8. Difficult to pull off

You can see from the columns above that both are necessary, but many leaders have become far too preoccupied with only putting on sizzling events. Events slowly fade in our memories and really don't change us. They sizzle and then they fizzle. This happens at big conferences, assemblies, retreats, rallies, summer camps, and concerts.

You would have enjoyed listening to Hank (not his real name). He was a dynamic speaker who pastored a church for most of his career. Three years ago, I attended Hank's funeral. It was a bittersweet experience for me, because I was among many people who loved his unforgettable style, his gimmicks for amusing a congregation, and his infectious laugh. But Hank acknowledged something to me, just before he passed away. He told me he was afraid he hadn't really changed anyone's life.

Wow. That's quite a confession—especially for a pastor. In a melancholy conversation, he grieved about how his life was spent "just holding a bunch of meetings." People liked to hear him communicate, but once the engagement was over, he couldn't point to any lasting change he'd made. He told me he tried to adjust his ministry style, but it was too little too late. He feared he had led a mere "preaching station."

While I'm not sure Hank's evaluation of his life is totally accurate, his "confession" became a wake-up call for me. I don't want to feel that way or say those kinds of things when I'm through. I don't want to only make a splash.

THE DIFFERENCE?

While I don't mean to diminish the value of a good speaker, I think most of us would admit that mere speaking events don't really change people. Many leaders step on the platform and simply make a splash. Nothing really changes. Real leaders make waves. Splashes energize. Waves catalyze. Splashes entertain. Waves equip.

Legendary evangelist Billy Graham knew that if his preaching ministry was to have any lasting effect on the people who attended his crusades, he'd have to establish a plan to collaborate with local ministries that made disciples after folks made decisions. He didn't want to only make a splash when he came to town. He wanted to make waves.

Let me attempt to summarize the difference between splashes and waves:

SPLASH LEADERS	WAVE LEADERS
1. Usually offer glitz and glamor	1. Always offer substance and depth
2. Make noise and gain attention	2. Make a difference and gain retention
3. Make a big first impression on people	3. Foster steady growth in people
4. Contribute to a great event	4. Contribute to a life-changing process
5. Think short-term impact	5. Think long-term influence
6. Big flash overnight	6. Big change over time
7. Transactional	7. Transformational

It may go without saying, but Jesus spoke to big crowds, and I'm sure his teaching was memorable. After all, we still read his words today. But the majority of his time was spent with a handful of team members (disciples) who lived close to him day in and day out. Jesus invested in them through the daily grind. He showed them how to live in every circumstance. What started with a handful of people has grown to become the largest faith movement on Earth. He told us it would work this way—like a small seed that over time grows very large.

Let's Trade in Glitz for Growth

Unfortunately, we live in a day of events and celebrities. We love the excitement of a huge crowd, with bands, lights, smoke, and great speakers. That will probably always be true. In today's world, however, where it's difficult to "wow" an audience because so many messages compete for our attention, let's remember the power of the wave.

There's nothing wrong with a leader who can make some splashes. We need those who can energize an event and motivate an audience. But we desperately need leaders who make waves and actually move people to establish new habits and attitudes. The wave is about growth, and growth generally happens in a developmental relationship with a mentor.

During the 18th century, George Whitfield and John Wesley were contemporaries. Both ministered to the British population at a time when the Anglican Church needed a shot in the arm. Both men traveled and preached outside, serving people who might not darken the door of a church building. In retrospect, Whitfield was actually a better orator, with a booming voice and a challenging evangelistic message. He preached to thousands of miners on hillsides across England.

John Wesley, however, organized his converts into small groups and equipped them to hold each other accountable to live holy lives and to grow in grace and truth once he rode away on his horse. So methodical was Wesley, that they called him the "great Methodist." He is the founder of the Methodist church. George Whitfield acknowledged Wesley's incredible contribution to Christian faith late in his life when he said, "My brother Wesley has chosen the better part. For he knows where his converts are and what they are doing. Mine are a rope of sand."

Splash leaders introduce great moments. Wave leaders introduce great movements.

Look at the Book: Reflect and Respond

Jesus described the growth of God's Kingdom as a small seed:

> Jesus put before them another parable: "The kingdom of heaven is like a mustard seed that a man planted in his field. Although it is the smallest of all seeds, yet it grows into the largest of garden plants and becomes a tree, so that the birds of the air come and nest in its branches." (Matthew 13:31-32)

1. What are the implications of this description? What can we infer about the size and speed of Kingdom expansion?

_____

_____

2. Why does this fly in the face of most American ministry or church growth models?

_____

_____

Assess Yourself

Reflect on your vocation. Circle the answer that accurately describes you:

When planning ministry events...

1. I put as much time into preparing for the follow up as I do for the event itself:

   NEVER   INFREQUENTLY   SOMETIMES   FREQUENTLY   ALWAYS

2. I care as much about the steady, spiritual growth of the audience as I do about the immediate response of the audience:

   NEVER   INFREQUENTLY   SOMETIMES   FREQUENTLY   ALWAYS

3. I place more value in the results of the event than I do the programming success of the event:

   NEVER   INFREQUENTLY   SOMETIMES   FREQUENTLY   ALWAYS

Try it Out: Practicing the Truth

Before your next speaking event, review the passage above from Matthew 13:31-32. Then, evaluate the planning of your event in light of Jesus' description:

1. Are you okay with starting small?

2. Can you embrace slow, steady growth?

3. Can you wait for the fruit (results) of your work?

Take a moment and journal about how you usually measure your success. In the past, have you been more about being a great speaker than about prioritizing steady growth from attendees? Take a moment and honestly evaluate your personal style. Share your thoughts with a friend. Then, talk about how you can improve.

The Marathon Problem

EVERY MARATHON HAS PARTICIPANTS AND SPECTATORS. THERE ARE FAR FEWER PEOPLE WHO ACTUALLY RUN IN A MARATHON THAN THERE ARE FANS WHO WATCH THE RACE. THIS IS A PICTURE OF MOST ORGANIZATIONS—A FEW DO MOST OF THE WORK. LIFE-GIVING LEADERS MOBILIZE THE MANY.

You've probably met someone who's run in a marathon. Several cities host them on a yearly basis. The first modern marathon was held in 1896 at the Olympic Games in Athens, Greece. The Boston Marathon started a year later in 1897.

Because it's such a long, brutal race—a little less than twenty-six and a half miles long—not everyone participates in it. There are tens of thousands who watch, but a smaller fraction who actually run the course. In short, there are lots of attendees but fewer participants. At best, those who watch are handing cups of water to the runners to keep them hydrated. They clap, they cheer, they observe—but they don't run.

The same is true for a basketball, baseball or football.

Every game has two components: first, there are a handful players on the field in desperate need of rest. Second, there are thousands of people in the stands in desperate need of exercise. It's true. After all, spectating is so much easier than participating. Players have to put in an incredible amount of work to be out on that field—the fans just show up. It's what I call the marathon problem.

So, why are there far more fans than participants? Oh, there are lots of excuses:

- "I'M NOT GOOD ENOUGH."
- "I'M TOO OLD."
- "I'M TOO YOUNG."
- "I'M NOT FAST ENOUGH."
- "I'M NOT STRONG ENOUGH."
- "YOU'D NEVER WANT ME TO PLAY."
- "I JUST ENJOY WATCHING A GOOD GAME."

Now, consider most non-profit organizations. They often experience the same issue.

Most ministries begin with a person—someone who's caught a vision to meet a need. They go after that vision and start meeting that need, which then creates a buzz. The leader collects stories to tell, and soon, others want to jump on board. Sadly, however, most initiatives never get past a handful of people. Organizations generally struggle once they reach a certain point where the central leader can no longer keep his or her finger on the pulse of the action. They often don't want to let go. Doing the work is why they started in the first place. The others who come end up as spectators.

- Church services
- Bible studies
- Campus ministries
- You name it

What Happened to Us?

Did you know that as of this book's publishing date, the average size of an American church is 124.[11] Why so small? (It can't be that every church is simply in a small town—many are in larger communities and cities). Nope. While I've not inquired of every pastor across our nation, I have a hunch as to why most churches are this small. I think this size is approximately how many people a single full-time pastor can care for. A single leader can shepherd about 124 people. Once you grow past that, more leaders are required. More participants, if you will.

But according to the late missiologist Peter Wagner, that means the "shepherd" must become a "rancher." They must recruit and equip other leaders and ministry staff to help serve the people.[12] And that requires a whole different skill set.

Far too often, we condition church members to be passive and watch our service. We request that they clap and give money. It's like a show. A performance. Think about how most view church in our country. It's an event they attend on Sunday. We call it a service, but that means sitting, singing, and listening. There is certainly no service involved. The average person is passive not active.

Ugh. But, this was never how it was supposed to be.

Another reason for the small size is that most people actually want to passively watch and not participate. At least, they think they do. (I actually believe that once people begin using their gifts and serving others, they catch the "virus" and never want to merely watch again. Alas, most never get up and try.)

People desperately need the spiritual exercise, but good luck getting them to risk it. They're far too eager to allow the professionals to do it. For too long, we unwittingly sent the message that professional ministry staff are the only ones qualified to serve.

I remember attending church as a kid. Church members called the ministers "clergy" and the members "lay people." The lay people might volunteer occasionally, but they were not qualified to do much. They were mere laity. Then, in college, I discovered the Latin roots for these two words and was stunned.

> THE LATIN ROOT FOR "CLERGY" IS "ECCLESIA." IT WAS THE SAME WORD USED FOR "CHURCH." THE PROFESSIONAL MINISTERS UNINTENTIONALLY ACTED AS IF THEY WERE THE CHURCH. THE LATIN ROOT FOR "LAITY" IS THE SAME WORD WE USE FOR "IDIOT."

Quite accidentally, over time we had the church and the idiots meeting every week. It's no wonder we never finished the work we've been given to do by our Lord. There were relatively few folks actually participating in the work. It all had to be done by professionals. Just like a marathon or a ball game.

Chicago Cubs Manager Leo Durocher once said, "Baseball is like church. Many attend. Few understand." Yep. That's about the size of it.

WHAT JESUS INTENDED FOR US

Good leaders find ways to plug people into appropriate places of active service; they help others own the mission; they are both mobilizers and catalysts. They build a new mindset into everyone involved:

- THE PARTICIPANT STOPS ASSUMING THEY MUST BE THE ONLY ONES TO SERVE.
- THE SPECTATORS STOP ASSUMING THEY CAN ONLY WATCH AND BEGIN TO SERVE.

For healthy ministry leaders, attendance is only the beginning. The ministry can be described as a funnel, with many people entering the funnel at the top and fewer actually reaching the bottom—but everyone is encouraged to go deeper than mere attendance. After all, this is not supposed to be a marathon.

FUNNEL DIAGRAM

OF PARTICIPANTS

MORE

ORIENTATION EVENTS

INVOLVEMENT EVENTS

SERVICE EXPERIENCES

LEADERSHIP

LESS

MULTIPLICATION

As people enter your ministry, they generally do so at the top of the funnel. So, events should be designed to attract an entry-level person who's just getting acquainted with your mission.

Following the attraction level are involvement level events formed to invite attendees into relationships and community.

Deeper are service level experiences that invite people to begin using their time and gifts to minister in some way.

Further still are leadership level experiences that challenge people to grow from serving to actually leading the service.

Finally, the deepest level is the multiplication level where people are leaders of the leaders. Each level of this funnel requires a "bridge" that carries (prepares or equips) people for the next level.

You Have to Coach and Train

In order to prepare those you lead for such personal growth and involvement, we must offer training experiences. Otherwise, the average person will never take the plunge. Equipping can be done OJT (On-the-Job Training):

- Watch you at first
- Then, you do it together with them
- Later, they do it while you watch
- Finally, they do it while you multiply in someone else

But you must be intentional about it. Jesus did this with his twelve disciples. He formed groups of disciples (70), then apostles (12), and down to his three closest leaders: Peter, James, and John, who had exclusive ministry experiences with him. I believe this was all deliberate on his part. He was a trainer. He gave fewer hours to spectators and more to participators.

We must build organizations that organically invite people:

- Into a circle, not just a row
- Into preparing for service, not just a show
- Into experiences that mobilize, not just motivate
- Into identifying what they can give, not just what they like to receive

When I served college students in San Diego, Richard entered our department as a shy and quiet young adult. After getting acquainted, I felt he'd make a great small group leader, so I asked him about it. He refused. He didn't feel qualified to do it. However, when I persuaded him to join a group (promising he didn't even have to say anything profound) he agreed.

All semester, he built friendships. In December, I asked if he'd be willing to serve as an apprentice. He wouldn't have to lead the group each week, just send reminders to attendees about snacks and meeting times. He agreed. Twice during that spring, the group leader was out of town, and Richard had to take over. He was brilliant. The next fall, Richard was leading a small group. Within two years, Richard was leading all the small group leaders.

Mission is almost always meant to multiply, to snowball, or accumulate. Everyone qualifies. It's about becoming participators not spectators.

LOOK AT THE BOOK: REFLECT AND RESPOND

In Matthew 9:37-38 Jesus said, *"The harvest is plentiful, but the workers are few. Ask the Lord of the harvest, therefore, to send out workers into his harvest field."*

1. Notice that the "marathon problem" was happening even then. What did he ask his disciples to do first?

   _____

   _____

2. Now, notice what he does next with his twelve. Read Matthew 10:1. Write down how Jesus enlists his closest companions to answer his prayer request.

   _____

   _____

ASSESS YOURSELF

We, as ministry leaders, must progress through four stages:

- DOING—We do all the work ourselves

   _____

   _____

- DUMPING—We get frustrated and dump work on others

   _____

   _____

- DELEGATING—As people avoid our dumping we learn to plan and delegate tasks

_____

_____

- DEVELOPING—Finally, our ultimate work occurs when we develop others as we offer them ownership of the work

_____

_____

Evaluate yourself. Write down what level you normally operate on, describing what you often do, and the steps you'll take to move people from consumer to contributor.

TRY IT OUT: PRACTICING THE TRUTH

Review the funnel diagram in this chapter. Do you have sufficient events and outlets for each level? Do you offer enough equipping opportunities to coach people to grow deeper in their participation with your ministry? Jot down your game plan to build out your own funnel and what training (and encouragement) you could offer those who hope to participate more deeply. What steps will you take to get better? Take a moment and journal about how you'll measure your success.

Teflon or Velcro

EVERY LEADER COMMUNICATES, BUT NOT EVERYONE GETS THE MESSAGE THROUGH TO LISTENERS. EFFECTIVE LEADERS ARE LIKE VELCRO. THEY CHOOSE LANGUAGE THAT CONNECTS, STICKS, AND IS NOT QUICKLY FORGOTTEN. THEY USE METAPHORS AND COLORFUL, UNIQUE TERMS THAT TEAM MEMBERS WILL GRASP AND REMEMBER.

I bet you've used pots made of Teflon as well as fabric that includes Velcro. Both are pretty common in today's world. Perhaps you'll enjoy a little background. Modern non-stick pans are usually coated with Teflon (polytetrafluoroethylene or PTFE). Roy Plunkett discovered it spontaneously in 1938, when he worked on a project with the DuPont Company. Believe it or not, the substance was first used in the development of the atomic bomb during World War II. It was valuable because of its unique corrosion-resistant properties.

By 1951, DuPont was solving some chemical problems with Teflon so that it could be used for other purposes as well. Soon, it was primed for discovery. A few years later, Marc Gregoire, a French engineer, was coating his fishing gear with Teflon, when his wife suggested using it to coat her pots and pans. A cookware revolution was about to take place. The Tefal Company was launched in 1956 to manufacture these non-stick pans.

Pretty slick, huh?

Velcro, on the other hand, was invented by a man name George de Mestral in the 1940s while hunting in the Jura Mountains of Switzerland. George was a Swiss engineer who discovered the tiny hooks of the Cockle Burs were getting stuck on his trousers and in his dog's fur. He studied them to discover how they attached themselves so well. Shortly afterward, he re-created the hooks with nylon material that made two fabrics stick. He called his invention Velcro—a combination of the words "velvet" and "crochet"—and formally patented it in 1955. Now, it's everywhere.

Pretty catchy, huh?

How Does This Inform our Leadership?

In short, Teflon is known for being slick so that nothing sticks. Velcro is known for being textured so that everything sticks. In the same way, a leader's communication will either stick with those they lead long after they've spoken, or it'll be forgettable. They'll either have "hooks" for team members to grab onto and remember, or they'll be ideas that fail to attach to anyone. They will slip from their memories.

We've all experienced both, haven't we? Reflect on times when people have spoken to you. Can you remember leaders who droned on and on, using loads of words, yet, it's hard to remember any of them? Conversely, can you recall leaders who find ways to grab listeners with their words and embed them into their minds and hearts? One is Teflon. The other is Velcro.

Now the important question is: which best describes your communication?

Growing up, I remember watching Dr. Martin Luther King, Jr. give speeches on TV. News programs would show clips of him speaking after a civil rights march or demonstration. He always had a way of crystallizing his thoughts into a memorable idea for listeners. He chose his words carefully and left people thinking every time he spoke. He inspired us. His words breathed life into his listeners. Dr. King found ways to make his ideas stick like Velcro.

The Ideas of Life-giving Leaders Are Velcro Not Teflon

One tangible way leaders can be life giving is through our messaging. What and how do we communicate? Do we breathe life into others with our words? Or, are our words empty and fail to accomplish our intent?

Each of us receives over 10,000 messages each day, via social media, conversations, email, TV, radio, phone calls, and advertising. Take a moment to consider this. It's enough to exhaust me just thinking about it! As a result of this onslaught, teen attention spans have gone from 12 seconds in 2000 to 6-8 seconds today. Herbert Simon summarized the issue when he said, "A wealth of information creates a poverty of attention."[13] So, how do life-giving leaders break through the noise and enable their messages to stand out?

A Velcro Leader's Words Are:

1. Fresh—They are unique
Life-giving leaders find ways to share ideas—even old ideas—in distinctive ways. They find words and mannerisms that are fresh and current for their listeners. It's the difference between the usual, "Good job today," and the stark, "You were excellent leading that meeting. You were clear with the objectives and kept the conversation on track in the midst of lots of different opinions. Well done!"

2. Inspiring—They empower

To be life-giving, by definition, implies inspiration. The words spur others on to higher levels of performance. The key? Inspiration always follows aspiration. People are stimulated when your request is tied to a goal they aspire to reach. Former Prime Minister Winston Churchill always connected his challenge for the British people to sacrifice during World War II to their aspiration of living free from Nazi occupation.

3. Emotional—They connect with the heart

Great communication includes three elements: logos, ethos, and pathos. Logos is about the message itself. Ethos involves the credibility of the speaker. Pathos is an appeal to emotion, persuading listeners through the speakers' passion. It's the fire inside us. Dr. King's speeches included all three—they're logical, emotional, and embodied by Dr. King himself.

4. Clear—They offer specific direction

Messages that are full of passion but don't offer clear direction miss the mark. The motivation is temporary at best, failing to furnish what's needed to hit targets. Clarity brings energy. Clarity brings creativity. Clarity brings resources to listeners. In most political elections, the winner is the one whose message and vision was clearest.

5. Transferable—They are easy to share

Life-giving leaders utilize words, phrases, and imagery that are memorable and easy for listeners to pass along to others afterward. In fact, great messages are a paradox: they are sticky yet sharable. You keep them but can give them away. Think about TV commercials you still remember. I bet their message is both sticky and sharable.

6. Timely—They are relevant

I believe messages that stick the best are tied to what listeners are facing in the moment. Life-giving leaders are privy to current events, in tune with the feelings of listeners, and deliver words that are both timely and timeless for audiences to implement.

When I created the first *Habitudes* images, I tried to follow the rules of effective, life giving communication. The chapters are short and to the point. They're driven by an image, which touches the heart, not just the head, and makes the principle sticky. In short, our communication has a better chance of influencing people today if it is short, simple, sticky, and shareable.

Two Case Studies

A simple study was done on motivating kids. On Halloween night, researchers placed a bowl of apples on a doorstep next to a bowl of candy. In between them, a sign read: "You ought to take an apple." After a sampling of trick-or-treaters, researchers found the vast majority of kids took the candy. It was predictable. Children love candy.

Once the sign was changed, however, nearly half the kids took an apple. What did the new sign say?

It simply read: "What would Batman eat?"

Instead of communicating "obligation" the message was about "inspiration." It was an appeal to the child's aspiration—to be like batman. The same principle applies to life-giving leaders. Their messages are Velcro because they speak to the heart and hope of their listeners. They tie inspiration to aspiration.

Following the Battle of Gettysburg, two leaders offered speeches in memory of the soldiers who'd died in that Civil War conflict. Edward Everett gave a two-hour speech, and Abraham Lincoln offered a 2-3 minute speech. Afterward, Everett perceived Lincoln's life-giving words. He wrote Lincoln, praising him for his eloquent and concise speech, saying, "I should be glad if I could flatter myself that I came as near to the central idea of the occasion in two hours as you did in two minutes."

In reality, the speech contained 272 words, and took Lincoln 2-3 minutes to give. But we still memorize them today. I have no idea what Mr. Everett said in his speech.

It reminds me of *Velcro and Teflon*.

Look at the Book: Reflect and Respond

1. In Matthew 5, Jesus shares His "Sermon on the Mount" with his disciples. It has been called His most famous sermon. What makes it stand out?

_____

_____

2. Why are "Velcro communicators" so rare?

_____

_____

3. Can you recall a "Velcro message" given by another leader in scripture?

_____

_____

4. What circumstances make it difficult for you to be a Velcro communicator?

_____

_____

Assess Yourself

Evaluate your communication based on two grids below. Reflect on a central message you try to relay to others, and see if you include these important elements:

1. **Logos**: What's the content of your message?

_____

_____

2. **Ethos**: Do you have the credibility to give it?

_____

_____

3. **Pathos**: Do you have genuine passion about it?

_____

_____

In order to foster life change, life-giving leaders usually include three things in their message:

1. A **Point** for their head. What's the key idea?

_____

_____

2. A **Picture** for their heart. Can you illustrate it?

_____

_____

3. **PRACTICE** for their hands. What's an action step?

_____

_____

TRY IT OUT: PRACTICING THE TRUTH

Plan to practice the following changes as you interact with others this week:

1. Don't think **obligation**, think _inspiration_.
   Instead of telling people they ought to do something, why not inspire them to hit a target because they want to? Tie your words to their aspirations.

2. Don't think **descriptive**, think _prescriptive_.
   Instead of telling people every step to take toward an outcome, why not describe the outcome together and let them figure out the steps?

3. Don't think **inform**, think _interpret_.
   People don't need leaders for information, but for interpretation. Instead of being an informer, help them interpret how to think, not what to think.

Fountains and Drains

LEADERS ARE USUALLY A FOUNTAIN OR A DRAIN—THEY FLOW AND OVERFLOW ONTO OTHERS, OR THEY JUST DRAIN PEOPLE OF THEIR ENERGY. THEY EITHER REFRESH THE LIFE IN OTHERS… OR THEY DRY IT UP. DRIVEN BY GRATITUDE AND PERSPECTIVE, LIFE-GIVING LEADERS FOCUS ON EMPOWERING PEOPLE RATHER THAN EXPLOITING THEM.

You and I have experienced both fountains and drains over the years. Both have to do with water flow. The big difference? One is about water flowing upward or outward, perhaps in a city square or a garden. These are fountains. They are beautiful to see. They carry with them a positive connotation. They are flowing expressions of life that people love to watch and admire. Some of the most attractive places to visit have fountains positioned in a prominent place.

Drains, on the other hand, are about water flowing downward. They are an opening in the sink that sends water, and anything else in that basin, down the plumbing, through the pipes, and into the sewer. It's a rather gross picture. They often carry a negative connotation with them. We talk about "draining experiences" or people who "drain us of our energy." They are the opposite of fountains.

What's interesting is that both exist in that garden or city square. Every fountain that people take pictures of above the ground also has a drain below the surface of the water. You just can't see it, and the architects planned it that way. No one ever comes to look at a drain. They come to view a fountain.

My early years were spent in Cincinnati, Ohio. From time to time, my family would visit Fountain Square in the heart of the city. It was eye-catching. A large statue stands high in the middle and has flowing water streaming down on two sides. People would come and toss coins in the pool at its base, making a wish as they threw it in. Built in 1871, Fountain Square remains as a landmark in that downtown area. While I've visited it many times over the years, and I assumed it was always there, I never remember once looking for the drain.

This is a picture of leadership and teams.

Many leaders are like fountains. They flow and overflow into the lives of others... and because they do, they're attractive to people. When this leader's life touches another person, it is energizing. It is encouraging. It sparks new ideas. It makes people feel better. They are life giving. Dynamic. Satisfying. They overflow with appreciation for others. When you see a fountain leader, you immediately want to be around them.

Other leaders are more like drains. They're always preoccupied with what's wrong with their team or what they don't have or still need—and they drain the energy out of people. In fact, when you see these people coming, you tend to try and avoid them. They'll sap you of your optimism. They'll deplete your energy for trying new ideas with fifty reasons why they won't work.

In short, fountains are water going up. Drains are water going down. So, how do people move from being a "drain" to a "fountain?"

It's About Our Approach to Leadership

It all begins with perspective. Team members who are fountains focus on gratitude for what they have. They never lose sight of what others have done for them; they know they didn't make it this far in life alone. They're thankful for opportunities, mindful of helpful people, and spill that gratitude and optimism onto others.

Team members who are drains tend to see the darker side of life. They reflect on the past and have regrets for what might have been. They focus on missed opportunities or failures. Life seems scarce rather than abundant. They're consumed with fears, doubts, or shame and tend to drain others of energy.

Research done with people both young and old reveals very interesting conclusions on the role of gratitude. Author and researcher Dr. Robert Emmons of the University of California Davis believes he knows what gives life meaning: pure and simple gratitude.

Emmons' team found that people who view life as a gift and consciously acquire an "attitude of gratitude" experience multiple advantages.[14] Gratitude improves emotional and physical health and can strengthen relationships, communities, and teams. Some strategies to build gratitude include keeping a gratitude journal, learning prayers of gratitude, and using visual reminders.

"Without gratitude, life can be lonely, depressing, and impoverished," Emmons said. "Gratitude enriches human life. It elevates, energizes, inspires, and transforms. People are moved, opened, and humbled through expressions of gratitude."

Unfortunately, cultivating an attitude of gratitude isn't easy.

The Inverse Relationship Between Gratitude and Entitlement

Gratitude is, according to Emmons, a "chosen attitude." We must be willing to recognize that we are the recipients of an unearned benefit. This is especially rare today where social media encourages us to build quite a narcissistic worldview. We live in a culture that cultivates a sense of entitlement, and it's seen across generations.

Do you ever find yourself feeling like you deserve any good you receive? It has happened to me too. I've realized I have to fight against that sense of entitlement each day because it's contrary to the growth of a spirit of gratitude. Entitlement is virtually the opposite of gratitude: as I feel more entitled, my gratitude shrinks in proportion.

Research indicates that gratitude is not merely a positive emotion—it can improve your health, if cultivated. Research also indicates that people must give up a "victim mentality" and overcome a sense of entitlement. Think for a moment. When someone feels entitled to benefits, there's little need for gratitude: I don't need to thank anyone; I deserved the gift. In fact, these people are lucky to have me around. I'm amazing.

As I have studied emerging leaders and their struggles, I've found that gratitude can actually have a positive impact on so many areas of their growth: energy levels, motivation, mental well-being, academic achievement, healthy, lasting relationships, and dealing with tragedy and crisis. Why would anyone not want to adopt this mindset?

In our work with professional sports teams, we enjoy our partnership with the Kansas City Royals. General Manager Dayton Moore called up Salvador "Salvi" Perez to the major leagues in 2011. At a press conference, Perez was asked why he didn't demand more money in his contract. The moment grew a little tense as Dayton was sitting on the same panel. But, I loved the way Salvi responded. He smiled and said, "I'm just grateful to play on this team and help build a winning club." That's the spirit that earned him a World Series MVP and helped the Royals win it all in 2015.

How to Become a Fountain

The good news is, our Heavenly Father offers us the opportunity to be "fountain" leaders. We can become problem solvers, instead of problem finders. Here are seven elements fountain leaders possess:

- ENERGY—Even when quiet, they exude passion that energizes others

- EMPATHY—They can identify and feel what others are experiencing

- OPTIMISM—They are hopeful and see the bright side of every issue

- GENEROSITY—Their abundance mindset enables them give what they have

- SELFLESSNESS—They see the big picture and serve others before themselves

- EMPOWERMENT—They are confident and believe in others' potential

- ENCOURAGEMENT—They offer words that give courage to those around them

Below are some case studies in scripture of both fountain and drain leaders:

- SAUL: Intimidating and insecure; he always compared his status to the status of David.

- DAVID: Full of faith, encouraged his men, inspiring in conflict, and secure in his identity.

- MARTHA: Hectic, busy, and distracted; kept score on her sister and complained.

- MARY: Soaked in Jesus' words undistracted; later served extravagantly and sacrificially.

- PHARISEES: Kept the rules but were judgmental, critical, negative, and pessimistic with sinners.

- JESUS: Full of faith and healing, added value, saw the best in others, and gave hope to others.

Jesus even contrasts His style with others when he said, *"The thief comes to steal, kill and destroy. I came that they may have life and have it more abundantly"* (John 10:10).

As they interact with people, the motivation for spiritual leaders is always healing: spiritually, emotionally, physically, and socially. It's about the restoration of people. Healing is behind all Christ-like leadership.

DRAIN LEADERS

1. Discouraging to people
2. See the downside of problems
3. Live with doubts and pessimism
4. Motivate through guilt
5. People feel they don't measure up
6. Source of caution and fear
7. Driven by memories

FOUNTAIN LEADERS

1. Encouraging to people
2. See the upside of opportunities
3. Live by faith and optimism
4. Motivated through gratitude
5. People feel they can reach big goals
6. Source of life and possibilities
7. Driven by dreams

Two men were lying in hospital beds, both with terminal diseases. One bed was next to a window; the other rested further inside the room and kept the patient from seeing out of the window. As the two men talked each day, the man by the window would smile as he shared what he could see looking out the window. He described a park with kids playing on a swing set, an ice cream vendor serving families a cold treat, and lovers strolling along the sidewalk. This made him happy. In fact, each day, the man inside the room grew resentful that he wasn't able to see these things. Why couldn't he be next to that window? One day, the man by the window passed away in his sleep. After he was removed from the room, his angry roommate asked to be moved to the bed next to the window. When he was, he got the surprise of his life. He gazed out the window and found that it faced a blank wall.

Look at the Book: Reflect and Respond

We see hints of this truth all through the New Testament:

- Fountain leaders come to serve, not to be served (Mark 10:45).
- Fountain leaders lose their life in order to find it (Luke 17:33).
- Fountain leaders cherish struggles due to what they achieve (James 1:2-3).
- Fountain leaders are humble yet are eventually lifted up (I Peter 5:6).
- Fountain leaders go last and end up being first (Matthew 20:16).

1. What do we learn about Jesus' others first approach to leadership, when contrasted with the world's approach? Describe his upside down leadership style?

_____

_____

2. When Jesus contrasts Himself with the thief in John 10:10, he talks about giving people abundant life. Define how leaders can join him in this endeavor. What are some specific ways leaders can "breathe life" on people?

_____

_____

Assess Yourself

Take a candid look at your leadership style. Then, place an "X" on the point in the line that best describes your leadership:

1. When a problem arises, would people expect me to react with…

   |---|
   HOPEFUL SOLUTIONS   RESENTFUL BLAME

2. When interacting with people in conversation, I tend to…

   |---|
   CONTRIBUTE ENERGY   CONSUME ENERGY

3. When examining a program or project, I usually…

   |---|
   SEE WHAT'S WRONG   RECOGNIZE WHAT'S WRONG

Try it Out: Practicing the Truth

Emma served as the copy editor for her university newspaper. Each week, she edited articles submitted by fellow students for grammar, spelling, flow, clarity, and excellence. Usually, the articles ended up with a ton of red ink. Initially, Emma saw her job as spotting mistakes in articles. But as she grew into leadership, she began to understand her role was actually to improve the writers of those articles. She started to meet with students who wanted to learn and helped them learn from their mistakes, empowering them to be better writers. She stopped "draining" and began "flowing" life onto her peers.

This week, make an extra effort to see the bright side and find the good in every interaction you have with people. Ask yourself: what could I do or say that would breath life on this person? Then, practice being a good finder and a grace giver.

Culture and Customs

LIFE-GIVING LEADERS KNOW THE BEST WAY TO BUILD A TEAM EVERYONE WANTS TO BE A PART OF IS BY CREATING THE RIGHT CULTURE. WHY? BECAUSE OUR CONTEXT ALWAYS EXPLAINS OUR CONDUCT. GOOD LEADERS GROW THEIR CULTURE BY FOSTERING SUSTAINABLE CUSTOMS, STRONG VALUES, AND CLEAR LANGUAGE.

I bet you've traveled to another country. At this point in my life, I've trained leaders in fifty countries around the world and always enjoy learning something while I am there. From industrialized nations like England and Singapore to developing nations like Uganda and Sri Lanka, I usually enter with expectations and exit with lessons learned from the variety of ethnic groups on Earth.

One particular lesson has been especially helpful over the years. When I see someone behave in a certain fashion, I've come to understand there's usually a good reason for it. While we are all part of the human race, we come from different ethnic groups, backgrounds, paradigms, and environments.

For years, I've wondered why so many of the fastest runners in international competitions are from Kenya. For instance, at the 2011 World Track and Field Championships, Kenya won an incredible 17 medals in the middle and long distance running events. The U.S. only won three. In marathon running, Kenyans are even more dominant. In 2011, the world's top 20 fastest runners—in the world's most universal and accessible sport—were all from Kenya. Something is going on there in the Rift Valley, where most of Kenya's runners originate. So, what is it? It's context.

Virtually every successful Kenyan runner is from a poor, rural family. From an early age, they have to run everywhere. Daniel Komen, the world record holder for the 3000 m. race said, "Every day I used to milk the cows, run to school, run home for lunch, back to school, home, tend the cows. This is the Kenyan way."[15]

As I've visited dozens of countries, I have found that not only do cultures differ from each other, but those cultures vividly illuminated me as to why people behave the way they do. Some cultures are naturally happy, while others are more depressed; some are very passionate and expressive, while others are more quiet.

Some are calculated, precise, and time oriented and others are more relational, warm, and event oriented. I am not arguing that any people group is better than another. They are just different based on the culture in which they live.

CONTEXT EXPLAINS CONDUCT

The truth is, when people act a certain way, the environment around them generally fosters that behavior. Severe circumstances actually induce behavior. In short: context explains conduct. All human behavior has a reason behind it. Behavior is always solving a problem—whether in a healthy or unhealthy way. People act to ease their pain, to get an answer, to meet a need, or to resolve a dilemma. In fact, crime is often an attempt to meet a real need in an unhealthy way. The sooner leaders understand this fact, the better off we will be. It doesn't excuse bad behavior, but it does explain it.

A therapist once told me about a family she was counseling. The parents brought their six-year-old son in for an appointment because they were sure he had mental health issues. When they'd leave the house for any reason, the boy would become emotional and scream. He often withdrew from social settings and hide in the bathroom. He came out smelling awful, as if he'd wiped his urine or excrement on his body. After careful conversation, the therapist met with the parents and gave a diagnosis. The boy was not crazy. He had been abused when they visited his uncle and believed the only solution was to hide or become so repulsive, no one would touch him.

A tragic illustration of the fact that context explains conduct.

WHAT CONTEXT ARE YOU CREATING?

My question for you is this: when you look at the behavior of the people you are leading, what does it say about your own leadership? What does it say about the context that you've created?

Effective life-giving leaders prioritize the cultivation of a healthy context and culture in their organizations. Knowing that conduct stems from context, they create the right environment for each person to experience health because healthy things naturally grow. For years, I have appreciated the statement, "When a flower doesn't bloom, you fix the environment in which it grows, not the flower."

The context of your leadership is made up of two ingredients: your systems and culture. When an organization isn't healthy, there's usually a failure of one of these two things.

1. SYSTEMS—The processes you put in place to get things done. Systems are all about maximizing peoples' gifts and capacity to achieve their goals.
2. CULTURE—The atmosphere you cultivate to foster energy. Culture is all about peoples' growth and engagement in the mission.

In short, systems are about efficiency. Culture is about engagement. When your context isn't bearing fruit, you can almost always bank on the fact that you have failed to create an effective system and/or culture.

The Power of Culture on a Team of People:

- All teams have a culture, by default or design.
- People are carriers of culture, good or bad.
- Some teammates are more contagious than others.
- There are as many cultures as there are managers.
- The culture affects behavior more than anything else.
- Leaders must hire the culture they want in team members.
- There is a difference between culture and climate.
- A leader's job is to cultivate a healthy culture.
- They do this through their habits and attitudes.
- Effective leaders know that people ultimately do what they see.

Years ago, I spoke to pastors in Cairo, Egypt. One minister from the Coptic Church was telling me about how hard it was to grow his church in that Muslim country. There were economic challenges, government persecution, and difficulty obtaining resources and facilities. I listened and empathized with him.

Of course, his church was small—it was very difficult to lead a church in Egypt. Interestingly, the next day, I visited the "cave church." It was a body of believers that literally met in a cave that had been transformed into an amphitheater. It was huge. Each week it held 14,000 people and the Bible study I witnessed was all about grace. How can one church struggle and one church flourish in the same city? It's simple. Context. Each had created different assumptions based on the culture they built.

What All Cultures Share

In the "Assess Yourself" section of this chapter, you'll have the chance to evaluate the kind of culture you've experienced in the past. For now, I'd like to discuss three elements every culture shares. Reflect for a moment. When you visit another nation, you usually discover how different they are through the following elements:

1. Shared Values
In Peru, for instance, they value relationships more than time. It's not as important to start a meeting on time as it is to connect with others. In the U.S., while relationships are important, we prioritize punctuality. Different values.

What are your values?

2. Shared Customs

In England, people drive cars on the left-hand side of the road. In America, we drive on the right side. Neither side is better, they're just different customs. All countries have certain customs or traditions that perpetuate the culture.

What are your customs?

3. Shared Language

This one is obvious. In France, people speak French. In Germany, they speak German. Each country has a primary language (or languages) used to connect and communicate. This, too, perpetuates the culture, values, and lifestyle. Companies, schools, and organizations also have certain words and phrases commonly used that reveal their organizational culture.

What is your language?

These are the elements that create context—on accident or on purpose. We must remember: the context of a place will explain the conduct of its people. And the climate may change daily. I have a friend who visited a church because its pastor was known to be an amazing communicator. After the service, my friend left underwhelmed. The sermon was average at best. As he left, an usher asked how he enjoyed it. When he said the sermon wasn't what he expected, the usher encouraged the man to return on another week. The pastor had just lost his son in a car accident the prior week.

Context explains conduct.

LOOK AT THE BOOK: REFLECT AND RESPOND

Jesus taught us to love others as we love ourselves (Mark 12:31). I have always felt part of this verse's meaning is to love with context in mind. We give ourselves lots of grace because we know about the tough day we just had. We tend to judge ourselves with our heart and judge others with our head. It should be the other way around.

1. How do you believe this passage instructs us to remember context in other's lives?

   _____

   _____

2. In Matthew 7:3 we read these words: *"Why do you look at the speck of sawdust in your brother's eye and pay no attention to the plank in your own eye?"* (NIV)

   What is Jesus teaching us about the importance of context here?

   _____

   _____

Assess Yourself

Organizations experience a variety of cultures that can diminish the potential of a team. Look over the list of organizational cultures below and determine if you have experienced any of these "less than optimal" environments. Place an X on the dotted line to accurately communicate how much you've witnessed them.

DESCRIPTION	YOUR EXPERIENCE
Toxic Negativity sabotages relationships, trust, and results.	NO ----------------- YES
Distant People are guarded, superficial, and only go the first mile.	NO ----------------- YES
Fun Great context, but you wonder, "Are we productive here?"	NO ----------------- YES
Confused Staff goal is to look busy; team is not aligned or focused.	NO ----------------- YES
Stagnant Maintenance, not mission is the team goal—plateaued.	NO ----------------- YES
Stagnant Folks wander unsure and shoot themselves in the foot.	NO ----------------- YES

TRY IT OUT: PRACTICING THE TRUTH

This week practice asking "why" whenever you see someone do something you don't understand. When appropriate, ask them why they acted as they did. Journal what you discover from their answers. This simple exercise is eye-opening to most leaders. Discuss your observations with your team.

[Fish and Bread]

Fish and Bread

BEFORE JESUS FED 5,000 PEOPLE, HE TOOK THE BREAD, BLESSED IT, BROKE IT, AND GAVE IT AWAY. HE WILL USE THE SAME SEQUENCE WITH LEADERS: AFTER ACCEPTING THEM AND BLESSING THEM, HE BREAKS THEM BEFORE HE USES THEM GREATLY. THE BREAKING IS SIMPLY PART OF THE PREPARATION.

We all know the incredible story of Jesus feeding multitudes on the hillside. Most of the time, we remember it as a story of stewardship. This is because God took the small lunch that a boy brought with him and multiplied it to feed thousands of people.

God doesn't need big gifts, just surrendered ones.

I believe, however, there is a leadership lesson to be learned from the story.

When we examine more closely what Jesus did when he received the lunch, we notice a pattern. Note that before Jesus used the bread to feed the 5,000 people he...

- RECEIVED IT
- BLESSED IT
- BROKE IT
- GAVE IT AWAY

I believe this is also a vivid picture of how God works in our lives. It's the order Jesus uses whenever he uses us. He first receives us. He says, "Come as you are." There's no need to clean up first or perfect your performance. Like the lunch, we may not appear to be enough, but he takes us. Then, he blesses us. We immediately experience the unmerited favor of God, the blessing of his forgiveness, peace, and joy. It's incredible.

But then, he chooses to break us. This is the part we don't like so much.

Just like the bread, he finds it necessary to break us completely before he can use us significantly. My personal leadership experience tells me he needed to break me of several things:

- SELF-SUFFICIENCY—My belief that I can meet all my own needs

- SELF-PROTECTION—My fear, which leads me to close myself off to others

- SELF-RIGHTEOUSNESS—My belief that I always know what's best

- SELF-PROMOTION—My desire to make my own name great

Why do we need to be broken of these things? Because leaders often begin well, but because our egos lust for recognition, our ministry becomes about us—our platform, our followers, our podcasts, and our numbers. This is why Jesus said if we wanted to come after him, we must "deny ourselves, take up our cross and follow him." Brokenness leads to purpose, which then leads to determination.

Our brokenness is an initial step in our preparation to be useful.

If we've never been broken, it means we're unproven in God's eyes. We may not be trustworthy. Just ask Jacob. Do you remember his story in Genesis 32?

JACOB: PORTRAIT OF A BROKEN LEADER

Jacob met up with the Lord, and wrestled all night with him on Mount Peniel. God finally brought Jacob to the place where he could use him because of four factors:

1. He was alone with God
This time, he had no props or people or backup plans to fall back on. He was on the mountain alone with the almighty God to seek his blessing.

Do you get time alone with God?

2. He was hungry for God
This time, he wanted God more than anything else. He didn't want the birthright or favor he once fought for.

Are you hungrier for God more than anything else?

3. He was broken by God
This time, he wrestled and didn't win against God. He won a birthright and two wives. But now, God broke him at his strongest point.

Have you been broken?

4. He was honest with God
This time he didn't cheat. He was honest about his life. He didn't lie about his name or identity. He admitted that he was Jacob, meaning "deceiver."

Are you transparent with God?

5. He was blessed by God

This time, he finally gained God's blessing by submitting. Pinned to the ground, the angel said to him, "You have prevailed."

God's favor comes after the breaking.

At first, Jacob tried to win—he was used to wrestling and winning. He cheated and connived to get everything he obtained since he was born. However, this time, he was wrestling God. When the Lord touched his hip and put it out of joint, Jacob resorted to a well-practiced stunt: demanding he receive something. He wanted a blessing.

The angel asked him his name. Strange question. Yet, for the first time in twenty years, Jacob was honest. He told the angel that his name was Jacob, which means cheater, conniver, supplanter. The angel responded strangely again. He said, "You have prevailed."

But how could this be? Jacob was on the bottom, not the top. That's how it works. When we finally allow God to break us of our "self-life," we win. We prevail when we finally lose by submitting to him. Victory begins with surrender. Take other biblical figures as examples:

- ABRAHAM HAD TO BE WILLING TO SACRIFICE ISAAC
- JOSEPH HAD TO SPEND TIME IN A PIT AND A PRISON
- MOSES HAD TO SPEND YEARS IN THE WILDERNESS
- DAVID HAD TO HIDE IN CAVES WHILE RUNNING FROM SAUL

HOW IT LOOKS TODAY

I remember two specific times during my career that God broke me. He used people and some tragic accidents to do it. In 1985, I was leading a college department, and we experienced a huge split in the group. A couple dozen students revolted against the direction we were taking. My leadership was questioned, and I was stunned. I grew quiet and barely spoke to my wife for two weeks. I was crushed. I felt betrayed. But God used that to take me to the wrestling mat until I finally surrendered. He broke me of my self-sufficiency (dependence on my gifts of communication and leadership), until I learned to lean completely on him.

The second breaking happened following seven tragic accidents. Over the course of five years, I was in six car crashes and one plane crash. In three of them, I was fortunate just to have survived. My car was smashed into an accordion in two of these accidents, and the plane crash I mentioned earlier in this book turned out to be a hidden opportunity from God. Four of us dropped 120 feet from the sky, spiraled down, and hit the ground. We were shaken up, but miraculously, we all survived. It was a time of soul-searching for me in the aftermath of that crash, but I emerged more focused and passionate about my calling. I became more urgent about the work I felt called to do.

Since that time, I've come to believe brokenness can be voluntary or involuntary. We can seek God's breaking and remain in a posture of humility—or we can do our own thing, requiring him to intrude and bring us to our knees. In Psalm 51:17 David wrote these candid words in a song to God:

> *You do not delight in sacrifice, or I would bring it; you do not take pleasure in burnt offerings. My sacrifice, O God, is a broken spirit; a broken and contrite heart you, God, will not despise.* —Psalm 51: 16-17

YOUR GOD IS TOO SAFE

In 1953, J. B. Phillips wrote a book called "Your God is Too Small." More recently, Mark Buchanan wrote a book called "Your God is Too Safe." It was directed at those who've unwittingly tamed God. We want him to help us but not control us. We prefer a domesticated God who rescues us, but doesn't require surrender. Unbroken leaders naturally seek a safe God they can utilize, not an unsafe God who controls us. I've observed the symptoms of leaders who follow this unreal image of God:

Truths We Must Embrace About the Safe God

1. When safety is our goal, we grow weary of being both compliant and defiant.

2. When safety is our goal, we get stuck in a "borderland," which calls us to be nice, but offers no power or insight to really follow Jesus.

3. When safety is our goal, we choose a life of maintenance rather than adventure. We play only defense, not offense.

4. When safety is our goal, we select a "safe god," not realizing he's our worst enemy. He breeds cowardice, steals joy, and keeps you stuck, complacent, and bored

Truths We Must Embrace About the Unsafe God

1. God's goal is not to advance our career, make us happy, or keep us safe. His goal is to advance his kingdom, make us holy, and draw us close to him.

2. God will take away the refuge of the familiar to beckon us to risk our lives following him in reckless abandon.

3. The unsafe God uses the element of mystery to capture our faith and imagination. Faith isn't a puzzle to be solved, but a mystery to be pursued.

4. God doesn't call us to be true to ourselves, but to deny ourselves, to come to what Galatians 2:20 describes as "the end of 'me.'"

It's interesting to note that even non-Christians recognize the need to be broken of self. Ernest Hemingway wrote, "The world breaks everyone. And afterward, many are strong in the broken places." Albert Einstein noted, "There is only one road to human greatness. That road is suffering." So, Jesus gave us a picture with the bread years ago. To nourish the crowd, the bread had to be surrendered (by the boy) and broken (by Jesus).

I see that pattern as necessary for life-giving spiritual leaders.

LOOK AT THE BOOK: REFLECT AND RESPOND

In Isaiah 6:1-8, the prophet Isaiah encounters God tangibly for the first time. Notice his first words are not a request for blessings or even a song of praise. He said, *"Woe is me, for I'm ruined. I am a man of unclean lips and dwell among people with unclean lips."*

1. Reality struck him. Isaiah saw the distance between him and God. Has this happened to you? When has God broken you of the "self-life?"

   _____

   _____

2. In his work with Simon Peter, Jesus revealed that he often must break us at our strongest point. Peter's fishing profession is called into question (Luke 5:4-5), and his courage is challenged (Matthew 26:33-34). Why do you suppose this is?

   _____

   _____

3. Why do you suppose God forces us to admit, *"I can't do anything"* (John 15:5) before we can say, *"I can do all things."* (Philippians 4:13)?

   _____

   _____

Assess Yourself

Respond to the four areas God often needs to break leaders. What's your story?

Leaders Must be Broken of:	Has God Broken You of This?
Self-Sufficiency	_____
Self-Protection	_____
Self-Righteousness	_____
Self-Promotion	_____

Try it Out: Practicing the Truth

Psychologist Rollo May once said, "Man is the strangest of creatures. He's the only one who runs faster when he has lost his way." Take some time and journal about why we tend to run from God's breaking process. Why do you, personally, tend to run from this process?

This week, pray the prayer of surrender. Ask God to do whatever he must do to break you and bring you to unconditional surrender. With a close community of friends, talk about your journey and how they can best pray for you as a leader.

Stethoscopes and Treatments

BEFORE PRESCRIBING TREATMENT, DOCTORS ALWAYS DIAGNOSE A PATIENT BY USING A STETHOSCOPE AND OTHER TOOLS TO LISTEN TO THEIR PATIENT'S HEART. LIFE-GIVING LEADERS APPROACH PEOPLE THE SAME WAY—THEY READ THEM BEFORE THEY LEAD THEM.

I'm sure you've made a few trips to the doctor's office in your past. As a Type 1 diabetic, I make several of them each year. I'll never forget getting diagnosed with diabetes in the fall of 1980. I was in college, and everything was going well. I was making good grades, playing sports, had some great friends, and served in a number of off-campus service projects. But that year, my body began doing some strange things. I became tired and thirsty all the time. I could hardly walk up a flight of stairs without stopping to rest. Then, my vision started going blurry. At that point, my roommate insisted I see a doctor.

It was then I got the news—my pancreas had stopped working. I was sent to the hospital and began taking insulin injections for my high blood sugars.

Along the way, I noticed the steps my doctors always took as they examined me. They'd look me over—my mouth, my eyes, and my ears. Then, they'd put a stethoscope up to my heart. Only after observing and listening did they prescribe a treatment.

I recently spoke to a doctor who told me he was taught in medical school to take at least ten minutes to diagnose someone before drawing any conclusions. In other words, good doctors read people before they lead people.

THE STETHOSCOPE OF A LIFE-GIVING LEADER

I believe good leaders follow the same path. They don't merely bark out orders for their team. Even when they know what steps must be taken, they take time to listen and to observe what's happening in the minds of their team members. Just like a doctor who already knows her patient likely needs an antibiotic, she'll still take the time to listen before speaking and observe before diagnosing.

One of the reasons this is necessary is because people send verbal and non-verbal messages to each other, and these messages all contain some subtext. Facial expressions often relay emotions. Body language communicates disposition. People tend to bring their personal lives with them to work. Good leaders function like a doctor, meaning that they lead after determining the backstory. They seek to understand before being understood. Just knowing that a person's behavior stems from both environments and temperament gives us insight. It's like using a stethoscope before deciding on a treatment.

THEIR BEHAVIOR SHOULD INFORM OUR BEHAVIOR

In a previous *Habitude*, "*Culture and Customs*", I explained that context explains conduct. The sooner leaders understand this principle, the better. In addition, this means we must choose our approach based on whom we are leading. Like good doctors, we must be able to "diagnose" our "patients." Wise leaders lead with empathy. We must feel, not just think, as we lead. And we lead based upon who they are, not just who we are.

Why is this necessary for effective leadership?

Empathy has been defined as the capacity to understand or feel what another person is experiencing from within the other person's frame of reference. It is the capacity to place oneself in another's position. There are many definitions for empathy that encompass a broad range of emotional states. However, for this *Habitude*, we will stick to three main types of empathy:

- COGNITIVE EMPATHY—THE CONSCIOUS DRIVE TO UNDERSTAND SOMEONE'S EMOTIONAL STATE

- EMOTIONAL EMPATHY—THE NATURAL DRIVE TO RESPOND ACCURATELY TO SOMEONE'S STATE

- SOMATIC EMPATHY—THE MUTUAL PROCESS OF BOTH PEOPLE MIRRORING THEIR EMOTIONS

In many ways, empathy is the opposite of apathy, which is to feel nothing. Pathos, a root word connected to apathy, is about passion. Apathy is about lacking passion. Life-giving leaders not only sense passion for their team's mission, but they feel it for their people.

"Having empathy also includes having the understanding that there are many factors that go into decision making and cognitive thought processes," Cindy Dietrich wrote. "Past experiences have an influence on decision making today. Understanding this allows a person to have empathy for individuals who sometimes make illogical decisions ... Broken homes, childhood trauma, lack of parenting and other factors can influence the connections in the brain which a person uses to make decisions."

In short, when leaders have empathy, they lead people out of a deep discernment of the factors going into each interaction. They lead beyond logic.

CASE STUDY OF AN EMPATHETIC LEADER

I'll never forget reading about Lieutenant Colonel Christopher Hughes. He was a commander of the 2nd Battalion, 327th infantry regiment in Iraq in 2003. When his battalion received a shipment of food and supplies for the Iraqi people, Hughes decided the best place to distribute it was the local mosque. So, he and his troops marched toward the house of the local cleric, the Grand Ayatollah Ali al-Sistani, to ask if he'd like to oversee the distribution. As the soldiers marched, however, locals assumed they were going to kidnap the cleric or bomb the mosque. A crowd gathered to stop the soldiers with sticks and rocks in their hands, ready for a fight. Two started throwing rocks at the soldiers. It was a tense moment.

That's when Hughes led with emotional intelligence and lots of empathy. He instructed his armed soldiers to stop, to drop down on one knee, to point their guns toward the ground and to look up into the eyes of the local Iraqis and smile. One by one, the locals began dropping their stones, and eventually, they smiled right back. Hughes avoided a conflict by leading with empathy rather than force.

Over my career, I have witnessed the disarming power of empathetic leaders. While they may appear to some as weak, they're actually strong. They display the strength to read a situation and do what is needed to make progress. In fact, I have come to believe these truths about our leadership approach:

1. There is not just one right way to lead.
Over the decades, universities that study leadership have evolved in their thinking. Good leadership is not reserved for the driven personality type that takes charge of the room. There are many effective approaches to leadership.

2. Effective leaders will change their style but not their principles.
Life-giving leaders know what can change and what must not change. Principles that make teams work are timeless: integrity, discipline, clear communication, vision, etc. However, our approach to a situation is based on whom we lead, when we lead, where we lead, and why we lead.

3. Lasting leaders choose their style by observing their people.
This is why successful, life-giving leaders are adaptable. Empathy—or reading the people and the situation first—informs the approach they take. After listening and observing the people around them, they wisely choose a relevant style.

Not only does context explain people's conduct, it should explain ours as well.

The Stethoscope of a Life-Giving Leader

Years ago, author Stephen Covey taught us in his book The 7 *Habits of Highly Effective People* that effective leaders "seek to understand before being understood."[16] For this reason, doctors take time to diagnose before treating a patient. As life-giving leaders, our methods should look much like theirs:

- Show me your eyes—What have you seen or experienced?
- Show me your ears—What have you heard that informs your behavior?
- Let me see your mouth—What do the words you have spoken reveal to me?
- Let me listen to your heart—What's going on inside that helps me understand?
- Where does it hurt—What pain (lack) do you feel that helps me to lead you well?

Years ago, I met an NCAA coach who grumbled at his young athletes who had little grit or stamina and felt entitled to perks beyond their scholarship. What's more, when he'd yell at them to toughen them up, they withdrew. They couldn't seem to take his shouting. He assumed they were wimps. During our discussion, however, we looked at the backgrounds of most of his young athletes. Until then, they'd always been the best on their team, they were seldom yelled at, and they were consistently told they were excellent, just for participating. While this did not get them ready for adulthood or college athletics, it did explain their actions. It also helped the coach develop a better approach for coaching his players.

The next season, he learned that when he began with empathy and then moved to expectations, he got the results he wanted. It required him, however, to seek to understand before being understood.

Too often, we fail to seek understanding and jump into the treatment, much like an incompetent doctor who rushes in to see a patient—without their stethoscope. The longer I've been a leader, the easier it is for me to make this same mistake. I've mastered my work, forgetting how hard it was to learn it. I feel confident; I have answers and assume I know what team members are feeling. Sadly, I can forget the basics of relationships.

Katy was a young girl who asked her father if she could play at her neighbor's house one afternoon. Her dad said yes but told her to return by 6 p.m. for dinner. When Katy strutted in the house thirty minutes late, her dad asked for an explanation. She simply said that her friend's doll broke. Her dad asked if she had been helping her friend fix the broken doll.

"No," Katy explained. "I was helping her cry."

LOOK AT THE BOOK: REFLECT AND RESPOND

Notice Jesus' model in Matthew 9:36-38: *"But when he saw the multitudes, he was moved with compassion for them, because they were weary and scattered, like sheep having no shepherd. Then he said to his disciples, "The harvest truly is plentiful, but the laborers are few. Therefore pray the Lord of the harvest to send out laborers..."*

1. When is it most difficult for you to use your "stethoscope" to better understand others? Are some personalities or situations harder for you than others?

_____

_____

2 Can you think of a time when you saw a leader demonstrate empathy? What was the outcome?

_____

_____

ASSESS YOURSELF

Circle the most accurate description of your leadership:

1. When team members fail to comprehend directions, I tend to...

   - GET IMPATIENT WITH THEM
   - FEEL SYMPATHY FOR THEM
   - BECOME DISTANT AROUND THEM
   - IMPROVE MY COMMUNICATION

2. If a teammate comes late to a meeting, I usually...

   - ASSUME THEY DON'T TAKE JOBS SERIOUSLY
   - WONDER IF ANYTHING IS WRONG
   - THINK THEY'RE UNDISCIPLINED OR UNREADY
   - ASK IF THEY'RE ALRIGHT

3. When a team member fails at a project, the first thing I think is...

   - "THEY'RE INCOMPETENT."
   - "HAVE I FAILED TO LEAD THEM WELL?"
   - "I PICKED THE WRONG PERSON."
   - "I'VE MADE MISTAKES IN THE PAST."

TRY IT OUT: PRACTICING THE TRUTH

According to Martin Hoffman, a psychologist who studied empathy development, everyone is born capable of feeling empathy.[17] Unfortunately, not all leaders possess an equal amount of it. Each day this week, enter your conversations with an imaginary stethoscope in hand. Ask questions and listen to peoples' hearts before assuming anything or giving directions. Jot down how others react. Discuss it.

The Golden Gate Paradox

AFTER A NET WAS PLACED UNDER THE BUILDERS OF THE GOLDEN GATE BRIDGE, CONSTRUCTION WAS FINISHED QUICKLY. LEADERS MUST BE DISPENSERS OF GRACE, ALLOWING TEAM MEMBERS TO FAIL FORWARD. THIS ENABLES TEAM MEMBERS TO SUCCEED MORE OFTEN AND MORE QUICKLY.

The building of the Golden Gate Bridge was a stunning feat in engineering. Bridge construction began in 1933, in the midst of the Great Depression. The unemployment rate was 25 percent, so people were looking for jobs. With the exception of some very specialized tasks, the bridge was built almost entirely by a local labor force. Workers were proud to be part of one of the most incredible achievements of the industrial revolution.

What you may not know is that the building of the Golden Gate Bridge is a story of astonishing safety standards. The expectation at the time for steel bridge construction during that time was one fatality for every $1 million in cost. By those standards, the safety record for the Golden Gate Bridge was impressive—losing only 11 workers for the $35 million project. How did they pull this off?

Typically, when someone fell and died during a bridge's construction, work actually slowed down because the remaining workers became apprehensive and fearful. Deadlines were missed, as the men became preoccupied with survival rather than success.

Chief Engineer Joseph Strauss was convinced, however, that although deadlines might be missed, workers needed to labor safely. So, Strauss made the site the first in America to have a $130,000 safety net suspended underneath the construction. The net saved the lives of 19 workers who called themselves the "Halfway to Hell Club." Not only did people survive, but also work sped up, as everyone felt empowered to focus on completing their jobs rather than be preoccupied with their own safety.

THE LEADERSHIP PARADOX

You might call this example a paradox. Suspending a safety net beneath a project costs both money and time. A leader might assume it's not worth the cost. Ironically, however, it saved time and money.

Similarly, life-giving leaders create an environment where team members are not afraid to fall, to falter or to fail. It's as though they place an imaginary "safety net" under the team. Suddenly, success comes more quickly because failure isn't final or fatal. The "net" empowers team members to succeed. They are concerned with doing the task well instead of simply surviving the job.

For several years now, our focus groups have informed us that today's young leaders have an extremely high fear of failure. In some ways, this is the fault of culture's message to young leaders: Whatever you do, don't make a mistake. Don't get it wrong. Don't fail. This may have left you with feelings of anxiety or the pressure to perform perfectly on every level.

A 2012 study posted in the *Journal of Experimental Psychology*, discovered this pressure might have a negative effect on learning. In several experiments, researchers found that students will perform self-protective acts and avoid any challenge where failure is an option.[18] Another study found that anxiety disengages the prefrontal cortex, a region of the brain that plays an important role in flexible decision-making. We have trouble making good choices. According to new studies published in *Educational Psychology*, "these students set the bar low, setting safe goals they're confident can be achieved. They're chronic underachievers."

Most leaders I know believe they have, indeed, created an environment where it's okay to make mistakes. Their team members, however, might say otherwise. My interviews reveal that too many students are absolutely horrified to do something wrong. They hold back by performing at below average levels, or they simply disengage. A 2015 report from *Gallup* shows 51 percent of the U.S. workforce is "not engaged" at work.[19] I believe part of the reason is that people feel they have no "net" beneath them. They don't want to fail so they don't do much at all.

What Could Your Team Look Like?

My guess is you've heard about organizations that practice the "Golden Gate Paradox" well. Years ago, I first heard of The 3M Company that not only encouraged risk taking, but they gave team members 15 percent of their week to experiment on projects they had dreamed up themselves. Chairman William McKnight would walk around, spotting employees working on unconventional ideas, and he would get excited about them, providing a sense of anticipation rather than anxiety. It paid off. Many of the products we use on a weekly basis were the result of this strategy: including Post-It Notes, masking tape, transparent tape, wet or dry waterproof sandpaper, and rubber cement. These were all created because the environment was life-giving and safe to make a mistake.

In *Habitudes for New Professionals*, I relay McKnight's basic rule of management:

> As our business grows, it becomes increasingly necessary to delegate responsibility and to encourage men and women to exercise their initiative. This requires considerable tolerance. Those men and women, to whom we delegate authority

and responsibility, if they are good people, are going to want to do their jobs in their own way. Mistakes will be made. But if a person is essentially right, the mistakes he or she makes are not as serious in the long run as the mistakes management will make if it undertakes to tell those in authority exactly how they must do their jobs. Management that is destructively critical when mistakes are made kills initiative. And it's essential that we have many people with initiative if we are to continue to grow.[20]

Thomas J. Watson was a pioneer in computing equipment and built a global industry during his 42 years as CEO of IBM. Part of his legend was how easily he embraced mistakes. In the 1940s, an employee made a mistake that cost IBM a million dollars. Knowing he would likely be fired over it, the man quickly typed up his resignation letter and handed it to Watson. The CEO responded, "Fire you? I've just invested one million dollars in your education, and you think I'm going to fire you?"

What an attitude!

Working under John C. Maxwell for 20 years, I had this same experience. John would tell us, "A person must be big enough to admit his mistakes, smart enough to profit from them, and strong enough to correct them."

CREATING SAFETY NETS TO INSPIRE TEAMS

To create this kind of environment, try this leadership path:

1. Offer the Gift of Clarity
Make sure those you lead understand what a "win" looks like. At the end of a project, what is the specific outcome you're shooting for? What is the clear objective? Ensure everyone is on the same page. People must be aligned and energized by the target.

2. Extend the Safety Net Principle
Let people know they have equal responsibility and authority to get their jobs done. Give them the freedom to try and make mistakes, while owning the project they are working on. Ultimately, they're free to fail, but must find a way to complete the task.

3. Practice "Try It Out and Talk It Over"
Team members feel safer to make mistakes and fail if they know they are free to try something new, record the results, and then meet with a leader to discuss the outcomes. As Jim Collins reminds us, "shoot bullets before cannon balls." Try out a small pilot project and see what hits the target before going big.

4. "Manage by Walking Around"

In this kind of environment, both creativity and mistakes will surface. You must be okay with both. You can minimize damage by practicing what Tom Peters calls MBWA: Manage by Walking Around—take a daily stroll to check out what's going on.

5. Recruit good people and trust the process

Once you get the right people in the right places on the team, do your best to trust the process you've created. While failure will happen, the price is worth it. Good things will be created and the benefit will outweigh the costs.

6. Ask the right questions to learn from mistakes

Instead of drawing conclusions or offering lectures, try leading with questions. Why did the mistake occur? Do they need more clarity and direction? Do they need extra support? Do they need the steps to be broken down? Be sure the questions communicate that you care and are confident in their abilities.

7. Express belief

This is the key action on your part. Be sure what you say and do relays belief in those you are leading. Discern what will communicate confidence, high expectations, and hope for them. Strong belief inspires strong behavior.

8. Follow through

Finally, whatever belief you've communicated, follow through in demonstrating its credibility. Don't undo what you've said with negativity or contradictory words. Be sure your actions match your words. This will help them "own" their work.

PLAYING THROUGH MISTAKES

Let me tell you about Roy "Wrong Way" Reigels. He was the NCAA football player who became famous when he picked up a fumble, and in his excitement, ran the wrong way toward the opposing team's end zone in the 1929 Rose Bowl. Roy was tackled by his own teammate, just before scoring for the other team. He got up, absolutely humiliated. He said later it was the worst day of his life.

What you may not know, is that during halftime, Coach Nibs Price said nothing about it. He gave an energizing pep talk and then said, "Alright, I want the same team to start the second half that started the first half."

Reigels couldn't believe it. In his disbelief, he just sat there, refusing to return to the field. With great discernment, Coach Price said to him as they sat alone in the locker room, "Roy, I believe in you. And, if you don't go out there and play this second half, everyone will remember you for what you just did in the first half. You owe it to yourself to show us all who you really are."

Coach Price said later that he'd never seen anyone play with more passion and intelligence than Roy Reigels did in that second half. He played through his mistake, but it took a life-giving leader with a safety net.

LOOK AT THE BOOK: REFLECT AND RESPOND

1. Religious leaders once brought a woman to Jesus who'd been caught in the act of adultery (John 8:2-11). Back then, the sin was punishable by death. When Jesus sends away the leaders, he tells her, *"I don't condemn you either. Now go and sin no more."*

   Talk about how Jesus offers a safety net but still challenges her to a higher standard?

   _____

   _____

2. What are the tangible benefits of a team that's empowered to make mistakes?

   _____

   _____

3. How can leaders balance freeing people to both make mistakes and make progress?

   _____

   _____

ASSESS YOURSELF

In raw honesty, place an X at the point on the line where you find yourself in your actions and emotions:

1. When I notice people making mistakes, I usually get preoccupied with...

   |--|
   OFFERING GRACE   OFFERING CRITICISM

2. As a leader, when things go wrong, I tend to...

   |--|
   BELIEVE THE BEST ABOUT PEOPLE   SUSPECT THE WORST

3. When I struggle with others failing on their tasks, it's usually because of...

   |--|
   THE LOSS OF PRODUCTIVITY   HOW IT LOOKS TO OTHERS

Try it Out: Practicing the Truth

This week, meet with your team and put some "safety nets" in place. Let others know it's okay to make mistakes on their projects. Then, follow through on the steps I offer in this chapter. Discuss the results by week's end. Was it a positive or negative week?

End Notes

REFEREES AND QUARTERBACKS

1. Pew Research Center, "America's Changing Religious Landscape," last modified May 12, 2015, www.pewforum.org/2015/05/12/americas-changing-religious-landscape/.

THREE BUCKETS

2. Yasmin Anwar, "Affluent People More Likely to be Scofflaws," Greater Good Magazine, February 28, 2012, https://greatergood.berkeley.edu/article/item/affluent_people_more_likely_to_be_scofflaws.

ROOT AND FRUIT

3. Stephen Covey, The 7 Habits of Highly Effective People, Coral Gables, FL: Mango Publishing Group, 1989.

4. iUeMagazine, "10 Warren Bennis Quotes On Leadership in Business," Last modified June 3, 2017, http://www.iuemag.com/u17/di/10-warren-bennis-quotes-on-leadership-in-business.php.

SURGEONS OR VAMPIRES

5. Positive Parenting Ally, "Diana Baumrind's 3 Parenting Styles: Get a Full Understanding of the 3 Archetypical Parents," accessed June 6, 2018, https://www.positive-parenting-ally.com/3-parenting-styles.html.

6. Daniel Coyle, "The Simple Phrase that Increases Effort 40%," last modified December 13, 2013, http://danielcoyle.com/2013/12/13/the-simple-phrase-that-increases-effort-40/.

7. Ibid.

CLEAN WINDOWS

8. St. Thomas University, "What is Situational Leadership? How Flexibility Leads to Success," last modified May 8, 2018, https://online.stu.edu/articles/education/what-is-situational-leadership.aspx.

SALUES AND SNUBS

9. James A. Roberts and Meredith E. David, "My life has become a major distraction from my cell phone: Partner phubbing and relationship satisfaction among romantic partners," Computers in Human Behavior 54 (January 2016): 134-141, https://doi.org/10.1016/j.chb.2015.07.058.

10. Brainy Quote, "Laurence Sterne Quotes," accessed June 4, 2018, https://www.brainyquote.com/quotes/laurence_sterne_165818.

MARATHON PROBLEM

11. Kelly Shattuck, "7 Starling Facts: An Up Close Look at Church Attendance in America," last modified April 10, 2018, https://churchleaders.com/pastors/pastor-articles/139575-7-startling-facts-an-up-close-look-at-church-attendance-in-america.html.

12. Peter C. Wagner, "Good Pastors Don't Make Churches Grow," Leadership Journal, Winter 1981, https://www.christianitytoday.com/pastors/1981/winter/81l1066.html.

Teflon or Velcro

13. Sparks & Honey, "Meet Generation Z: Forget Everything You Learned About Millennials," slideshow, last modified 2014, https://www.slideshare.net/sparksandhoney/generation-z-final-june-17.

Fountains or Drains

14. Robert Emmons, "Why Gratitude is Good," Greater Good Magazine, November 16, 2010, https://greatergood.berkeley.edu/article/item/why_gratitude_is_good.

Cultures or Customs

15. TLF Research, "What's the Secret?" Accessed June 4, 2018, https://www.tlfresearch.com/whats-the-secret/.

Stethoscopes and Treatments

16. Covey, 7 Habits.

17. Daniel Goleman, "Researchers Trace Empathy's Roots to Infancy," The New York Times, March 28, 1989, https://www.nytimes.com/1989/03/28/science/researchers-trace-empathy-s-roots-to-infancy.html.

The Golden Gate Paradox

18. Frederique Autin and Jean-Claude Croizet, "Improving working memory efficiency by reframing metacognitive interpretation of task difficulty," Journal of Experimental Psychology: General 141, no. 4 (2012): 610-618. http://dx.doi.org/10.1037/a0027478.

19. Amy Adkins, "Employee Engagement in U.S. Stagnant in 2015," Gallup News, January 13, 2016, http://news.gallup.com/poll/188144/employee-engagement-stagnant-2015.aspx.

20. Tim Elmore, Habitudes for New Professionals: The Art of Launching Your Career, Atlanta, GA: Growing Leaders, 2015.

Acknowledgements

Allow me to acknowledge and thank the team of people who made this book possible. I am grateful for the gifted people who co-labored with me:

Andrew McPeak who oversaw the production of this book. His eye for excellence and attention to detail insure its message is clear.

Jim Woodard, who oversaw the layout and acquisition of the photographs. Jim understands what we're attempting to do as we teach and learn through images.

Emma Smith, who was our copy editor. She labors tirelessly to insure the grammar and spelling accurately relay the truths of this book.

Colin Eurit, who researched both data and stories for this book. Colin has become a servant leader in his own right.

Matt Litton, who served as our primary line editor, offering not only edits, but also wise counsel to insure the message of this book comes through loud and clear.

Chris Harris who drove our team to focus on what makes this book unique and how we might vividly describe its value to readers.

Holly Moore, who empowers our team to be life-giving leaders by modeling the way.

Notes

Notes

Notes

Notes

Enjoy Habitudes?

Help us bring these lessons to students who can't afford them.

1/4 Young Adults *live in* **POVERTY**

8/10 Young Adults *plan to* **MOVE HOME** *after College*

In both urban and rural environments, **students are sheltered** *within a 9-mile radius of their home,* **shielded from experiences** *that involve risk or failure.* **This leads to delayed maturity.**

All over the country and in developing nations around the world, there are students who are not equipped to lead themselves (or others) into the next steps of their lives. What's worse, their schools can't afford leadership development materials to help them mature into the best versions of themselves.

We want to change that. We want to help students broaden their vision, take bigger risks, think bigger thoughts, and pursue bigger goals.

To do this, we created **The Growing Leaders Initiative**, to provide *Habitudes* in schools and youth non-profit organizations that cannot afford to purchase programs for their students. Thanks to donor support, grants are available for qualified applicants.

To apply or donate, visit
www.TheGrowingLeadersInitiative.com.